WAITING *for*
MORNING

HEARING GOD'S VOICE
IN THE DARKNESS

CINDY CROSBY

FOREWORD BY PHYLLIS TICKLE

Baker Books
A Division of Baker Book House Co
Grand Rapids, Michigan 49516

© 2001 by Cindy Crosby

Published by Baker Books
a division of Baker Book House Company
P.O. Box 6287, Grand Rapids, MI 49516-6287

Printed in the United States of America

Cindy Crosby, 1961–
    Waiting for morning : hearing God's voice in the darkness / Cindy Crosby.
        p. cm.
    Includes bibliographical references.
    ISBN 0-8010-1222-8
    1. Nature—Religious aspects—Christianity—Meditations. I. Title.
BT695.5.C76 2001
242—dc21   2001025033

FOR JEFF

CONTENTS

CONTENTS

FOREWORD

Some years ago, I had a dear friend who was a crack reporter for, and eventually the managing editor of, a large, metropolitan newspaper. Right up until the day of his death, Dan had a banner hanging behind his desk on which, in heavy pseudo-Gothic script, he had written: Someday I'm going to quit this job and learn to write.

Dan did not live long enough to act on that framed intention, but the desire it contained was always there; and though there was obvious humor and self-deprecation in his sign, its sentiment was no less genuine for him, no less a statement of the ideal toward which he always was yearning. In this he was not alone within the guild of accomplished journalists. Over my years as a member of sorts in that profession, I have known many, many reporters like Dan who, despite their obvious success in newspaper and magazine work, still wanted some day "to grow up and become a writer." The truth is that most of them never will, not because they will be cut off from their goal as he was by some premature interruption, but because, truth be told, they simply cannot fulfill it.

7

The "Who, What, When, Where, Why" questions that are the core of good reportage deal with the dimensions and phenomena of an objective world, their very crispness playing to the matter-of-fact and not to the mythic. The nuances of passage and connection between observable reality and abstract reality are, as a rule, the stuff of poetry and art, of creative writing and inspired thought, not of succinct reportage. Alas, too, the habits that train the mind to ask and answer the questions of dimensional time all too often come eventually to prevent it from asking or answering the questions of timelessness. Thus the poignancy for many a good man and woman of Dan Henderson's office sign.

Cindy Crosby is by trade a reporter. She is, in fact, a very good one. She is also that rare, rare reporter who is a writer as well. *Waiting for Morning*, her first book, is more than proof of that. Within its pages, the educated skill of the trained questioner and the soul of an observant Christian join forces to record the spiritual travelog of a woman who has traveled broadly in the confines of her own suburban gardens. With a reporter's reverence for precise details and a believer's reverence for the divinity behind every one of them, Crosby speaks with ease and affection and, ultimately, with great familiarity about the holy space that is the verge between those two ways of knowing. One can only hope that *Waiting for Morning* is just the first of many such reports from that place of the soul. In the meanwhile, however, it is enough simply that we should be grateful for this one.

PHYLLIS TICKLE

INTRODUCTION: COMING OUT OF THE DARK

One of the most basic laws of life is rhythm. Night follows day, winter follows summer, we wake and we sleep.

In spiritual life . . . there will be times of consolation and times of desolation.

JOHN ORTBERG

Several years ago, I found myself in the midst of a severe depression. There were several triggers: an unwelcome move, the loss of some good friends, the onset of a midlife crisis, family members who experienced debilitating illnesses. For the first time in my well-ordered life, I felt as if things were out of control. I was angry with God, unhappy with my husband, frustrated with my circumstances, disappointed with the way my life was turning out.

The one thing that seemed to help lift my spirits was taking long walks in the pockets of forest preserves and arboretums tucked into the new urban area that was now my home. A Christian from the cradle who had lived mostly a life of acceptance, I found myself questioning God. While I walked, I wrestled endlessly with difficult questions about my faith. For the first time in my life, I didn't hold anything back from God. I let him have it.

God seemed mostly silent. But as I spent time outdoors, in the mornings and the twilight, in warm weather and on freezing January afternoons, I began to pay attention to the world around me. I had always been an avid gardener and enjoyed nature, but my love of the outdoors had focused mainly on whatever real estate we happened to be living on at the time. Now, as I daily walked the trails and hiked the paths in the natural refuges I discovered in the city, I found myself distracted from my self-absorption by what I saw in the bigger world around me. I watched little dramas unfold: the shoots and leaves of bloodroot that poked up under the oak trees by the path, changing bit by bit into pearly petals that lifted toward the light filtering through the woods; the grasses on the prairie that started as insignificant green shoots and by fall were rippling plumed banners that waved over my head. The birds I saw and heard began coming into focus, and I found pleasure in learning their songs and their names. Animal prints on the trails suddenly stood out. I made a tiny garden in my backyard and watched my plants cycle through the seasons—sprouting, growing, flowering, and dying. As I sat on my porch late at night, I looked more carefully at the stars and became interested in the constellations.

Day after day, night after night, the God who I thought was silent revealed glimpses of himself. I saw that the God who methodically numbers the seeds in the sunflowers in mathematical sequence is also a God who allows random violence, such as a small mouse snatched from a path by a red-tailed hawk. The God who paints the tallgrass prairie in beautiful colors also allows wildflowers to be trampled and broken by deer as they make their beds to sleep. The God who feathers the cedar waxwing is also the God who lets a baby bird fall out of its nest, its body cold and broken.

Our world is a fallen one. We ride the roller coaster of good times and difficult seasons. Change and disappointment. Joy and exhilaration. Exhaustion and depression. Fulfillment. Spiritual dryness. Happiness. Suffering. Life comes at us in waves, a rhythmic series of events that sometimes pound us in the surf and other times take us for a smooth ride in the current.

We will never be completely at peace on earth; we will always be restless until we find the landscape of heaven. Yet, the landscape of earth is the framework God has given us to live out our lives. Indeed, he made the natural world before he made us.

Evelyn Underhill writes, "The teeming life of nature has yielded up to your loving attention many sacramental images of Reality." I began to realize that God didn't create the world— or my life—on a whim. Embedded in nature, he gives clues about who he is, inklings of how the Holy Spirit works, signs of his love and care for us. He also shows us how death and resurrection, agony and beauty, pain and perfection can all coexist in harmony and be woven into this tapestry we call life.

While learning about the natural world and its wonders, I learned about myself. Through the rhythms of nature, I began to see the rhythms of life, the ebbs and flows of the universe. I began to realize that the dark and the light both play a role in forming my spiritual nature. I learned to embrace both. There was peace that no matter how troublesome my circumstances, how trying my season of life, God is always with me.

By welcoming the dark and the light together, the visible and the invisible, I began to stretch and to grow—to experience anguish and disappointment in my life, yet not turn away from God, to lean toward the light and learn through the darkness.

So much is a mystery. All we can do is pay attention and try to understand as much as is offered, accepting what stays veiled, riding the roller coaster . . . sometimes with our eyes closed in fear, other times with our eyes wide open. Through change and difficult circumstances, we are molded, shaped, and formed, hoping to say as Søren Kierkegaard said, "Now, with God's help, I shall become myself." And learning to accept the sometimes painful and often exhilarating journey that gets us there.

LIFE AND THE BURPEE SEED CATALOG

Believing the Promises of Words on a Page

> Except the seed die . . . it has to die in order
> to liberate the energy it bears within it so that
> with this energy new forms may be devel-
> oped. So we have to die.
>
> SIMONE WEIL

Five years old. I'm camping out in my cave of arched forsythia, a blooming yellow tent of floral abundance that effectively hides me from the outside world. The shade under the weighted branches keeps grass from growing, giving me a polished dirt floor under my bare feet. I make myself more comfortable by dragging out my mother's best sheets from the beds inside.

In my backyard hideout, I can stay comfortably hidden until she calls for me to come and eat lunch. Today, it will be pickle-pimiento-loaf sandwiches, salty figured pretzels, and Dixie cups full of red Kool-Aid, all consumed on the blistering hot concrete back porch.

In the coolness under the forsythia, I am making dinner for my dolls. Grape hyacinths with their pearl-like amethyst clusters mixed with yellow dandelions make beautiful mock fruit salads. I dust everything with red tulip petals, then interlace a few toadstool umbrellas through it all for garnish.

My mother, with the prescience of all mothers, has warned me and my younger sister and brother not to eat anything that grows in the yard. When we cook, we content ourselves with concocting gourmet delicacies and pretending to eat them. "Very good," I say to my yarn doll Sally Dally, propped up next to me against a branch, a leaf plate on her knitted lap. I chew on air, smack my lips, and pick up another grape hyacinth's beady bloom. "My compliments to the chef."

We inherited this backyard when I was two years old, my parents purchasing it from an elderly Adam and Eve who created their own version of the Garden of Eden on a quarter-acre lot. Enamored with every nursery and seed catalog ever to pass through a mailbox, the first owners made their yard a paradise of perennials, attempting to plant at least one of everything that flowered, branched, or put out shoots.

As kids, my siblings and I plot the changing of the seasons by the changing of the yard. Fall brings ripeness to the Jonathan apples grafted on the crab apple trees and brushes the leaves of the pin oak standing sentinel in the west with burnt orange and deep sulphur. Winter means bare branches, and no hiding places unless we build a snow fort.

A pussy willow anchors one corner of the yard, its fuzzy buds a signal of the winter's coming demise. When my mother brings branches inside for forcing, we know the dark days are almost at an end. Spring is also heralded by the magical appearance of Dutch hyacinths in lavenders and blues, their heady fragrance tantalizing our noses. Tulips line up and bloom in orderly ranks along the fringes of the garden border—a jumble of dark plums, intense reds, plain yellows, and variegated whites with streaks of green. I know that school is almost out when ants blaze trails all over the peony buds, soon to unfurl in a shattering of deep coral, pink, and white—a conga line of big-bosomed showgirls in flashy costumes. Iris muscles in by Memorial Day, blooming in bearded blues and purples, rusts and lemons.

The smell of lilacs percolates through the humid, steamy air of late spring. There are three bushes, all higher than my head, each with a different color of spiky blooms: one deep purple, one light lavender, and another pure white. In the hot days of summer, parched grass crackles under our bare feet while scarlet Blaze roses clamber over the chain-link fence, draping it in crimson. The fragrant viburnum bushes yield summer "snowballs" that we throw at each other in mock battles, scattering a sprinkling of white over the deep green of the lawn.

Boston ivy mounts an assault on the bricked back wall of our house, flanking and occasionally snaking over the large, concrete-slab porch, which is the stage for childhood enactments of our favorite dramas. The obligatory blue plastic pool and garden hose cools us when July gets too scorching to bear, as does the sprinkler that monotonously rocks back and forth, back and forth, spraying us with moisture. Our yard is rimmed with crab apple trees, which provide green bullets of ammunition in summer for the staged skirmishes we wage with our bitter enemies, the slightly older twin boys who live across the fence behind us.

Luxuriant, untamed, overgrown—our yard was a magnet for the neighborhood kids. Floral-patterned bedsheet tents mushroomed under the oak trees. We plucked blooms and served them to our friends at imaginary restaurants under the shrubs. Red Flyer wagons carted around Barbies and GI Joes, who adventured in the sandbox and were married at staged weddings under the mauve flowers of the weigela bushes.

Bare spots in the grass showed where, after work, my dad would throw together spontaneous games of Whiffle ball. First base was by the big crab apple, second by the peonies, third by the pin oak, home base by the porch. He never minded the base paths we gouged out in the lawn.

My mother never said a word about the havoc we wreaked on the landscape, no doubt happy to have us occupied and out of her hair for a while. With three children spaced two years apart, gardening was the farthest thing from her mind. However, my father's mother, who was hyperconscious of social standing in the community, agonized over the way our yard wandered toward wildness. Every other year, she dispatched a crew of lawn and maintenance workers to our yard as a surprise "gift," and they whacked back the trees and shrubs into some semblance of suburban respectability. My parents tolerated this for the sake of peace, but I remember my mother's lips getting thinner and thinner, finally disappearing altogether as she fumed under the surface at this invasion of her life. She vented her rebellion by letting everything go back to wildness, and the cycle would start all over again.

The wilder for us kids, the better. The longer the branches, the more hiding places we could find. The taller the trees, the more there was to climb. Ours was the only yard in the neighborhood where someone's dad wasn't admonishing us to "be careful about my grass" or where we had to watch where we

19

played. It wasn't long before this diminutive Garden of Eden made me long to be not just a partaker but a creator.

When I was eight, my sister and I took piano lessons from Mrs. Hart, a petite, dark-haired woman who with weekly regularity ran us through the scales I rarely practiced. My half-hour session was first; then it was my sister's turn. In the deep high-backed armchair where I waited, I leafed through the Harts' magazines. While my sister plunked out "My Little Birch Canoe," I became wholly absorbed in the Burpee seed catalog that fueled Mrs. Hart's country garden. Pinwheels of multicolored ruffled zinnias paraded across the cover. Mammoth vegetables spilled over the stapled pages. Neon sails of lettuce. Brick-red globes of beefy tomatoes. Heavy clusters of green beans.

There was a centerfold of nothing but corn, half-nude ears slightly husked to show enticing rows of succulent sweetness. I rolled their names over and over on my tongue, savoring them. Sunglow. Carmelcross. Honey and Cream. Golden Beauty. Xtra-Sweet. Promises of paradise for only pennies a packet.

Interspersed among the familiar were odd vegetables I had never eaten—exotic vegetables to my Midwestern eyes, speaking of places not yet traveled. Crispy Choy Chinese cabbage. Hungarian wax hot pepper. San Marzano paste tomato. I dreamed of having a spot of my own where I could plant all the colors of this catalog cornucopia. I wanted to sample delights unknown from the limited produce selection at the local supermarket where we shopped, to travel virtually through vegetables to these distant places.

I appealed to my mother, who, long-suffering in all things, allotted to me a six-by-six-foot square flanked by a corner of the chain-link fence that abutted the neighbors' yard. After withdrawing nickels and dimes from my white cat bank, she helped me total my savings and place my first order from Burpee. Tactfully, she steered me to some tried and trues. Heavenly Blue morning glories. Charleston Grey watermelons. Black-seeded Simpson leaf lettuce. Cherry Bell radishes. Danvers Half-Long carrots. Gold Nugget marigolds. No exotics, but I was happy. A few Big Boy tomato plants were purchased from the local hardware store and thrown in free by Mom for good measure. Far too many seeds and plants for the small space I cultivated, but not nearly enough in my childish eyes to execute my fantasies.

With my cheap dime-store trowel and rake, I pummeled the rocky clay hardpan and turf into my field of dreams. I lined the base of the chain-link fence with morning glory seeds and marked rows for vegetables, then made two "hills" for watermelon and meticulously placed marigold seeds along the outside border. Everything was then deluged with the garden hose.

A week or two passed after I planted my plot, barely enough time for the morning glory shoots to crack their way through the earth. There was a misting of green from the carrots, and the tomato plants began rooting and opening a few timid yellow blooms in response to the warming of the earth. But I was impatient. I longed for my garden to look more like the pages of the catalog, less like a speckled green crater on the moon.

Late one afternoon, when my sister and I were lying on our stomachs on the floor of our room, going through our shoeboxes of Topps baseball cards and making trades (Catfish Hunter for Johnny Bench? Sal Bando for Pete Rose?), the door to the bedroom burst open, and my little brother came running in, breathless, shouting that the tomatoes were ripe. Ripe? I had looked at the tomatoes a few days ago, and only a few marble-sized green balls indicated anything was developing at all. A miracle had occurred! A gardening marvel, a freak of nature.

Unbelieving, my sister and I slid open the screen door to the porch and ran barefoot across the grass to the garden, followed by my brother. There, nestled in the crotch of the still-scrawny green tomato branches, was a mammoth, flaming-red tomato. I was astounded. How had I missed it the week before? How had it ballooned to this mature globe in a matter of a few short days? In jubilation I leaned over to pick it—my first tomato!—and hefted it in my hand.

It was—lightweight. It was—hollow. It was—plastic!

My brother doubled over in laughter, howling with the success of his joke. I threw the plastic tomato at him and it missed, lightly hitting the turf and rolling away. I spent the next few minutes chasing him around the yard.

I had better success with the morning glories. The seeds were perfect for a kid—large, easily handled, effortlessly placed into the holes. I watered them meticulously at first, and they responded by poking up green heart-shaped leaves and twining quickly up the chain link, almost quickly enough to satisfy my impatient gardening heart. I plotted their progress up the fence, until they reached the top and stretched yearningly into open space. Heavenly Blue crinkled blooms unfurled like parasols every morning, spritzed with raindrops of dew. My only disappointment was that they closed up by early afternoon.

Some of my other seeds didn't fare as well. The watermelons I planted languished, never living up to their catalog promise: "two feet long; twenty-eight to thirty-five pounds each!" My Charleston Greys were baseball-sized at best, no doubt thirsty for the water I forgot to give them as the summer wore on and I was diverted by more interesting pursuits: playing tag with my best friend next door, trekking to the library down the street for the latest Nancy Drew mystery, and catching butterflies in the meadow at the end of the block. The carrots likewise suffered from rocky soil and a lack of water, never developing past hairy, forked, thumb-sized orange spears. By the time I scraped off their rough, dirt-encrusted outer skin, they were barely slivers.

Despite my inattention, my diminutive square soldiered on by itself. The marigolds put out bushy fronds and bloomed in dark maroon and crimson, saffron and chrome. Lettuce put up some tentative leaves, which although bitter from lack of water and a surfeit of heat, were still borne proudly to the kitchen. My mom used them to garnish our bologna sandwiches, sneaking a few into salads at dinner. Radishes, the indispensable mainstay of every childhood garden, grew red and round under the dirt.

23

Other plants also flourished. Ragweed crept in, and I, off playing baseball across the street with the neighborhood boys, neglected to pull it. Dandelions, uninvited guests at the party, mingled integratingly between the marigolds, blooming yellow, camouflaged by color. Chickweed covered the garden floor like a lacy doormat.

Despite the weeds and the less than top performance of some of my vegetables, it was still a revelation to me to make the connection between the morning glories that twined on my fence, the scarlet globes of radishes, the fringed flowers of the marigolds, and the photos and descriptions I had read in the colorful pages of the Burpee seed catalog. I was amazed that I could read the words on a snowy January afternoon, then, by virtue of a few cents and a stamp, have seeds come to me in April, waiting in my mailbox. After I poked the seeds into our unforgiving clay—voilà! Beauty from an envelope. Life wrenched from the casket-like shells of apparent death. These seeds, these promises, brought to birth by my own will, my own two hands.

My garden was one of the earliest connections I made between dormancy and life, death and resurrection. What seemed tough and worthless could become something of value, something of great beauty, like those Heavenly Blue parasols with their diamond drops of dew. Without action on my part, however, the words on the page would have been meaningless. Unfulfilled promises. I had to lick the stamps and send in my order, prepare the ground, and water it. Even then, the results weren't always what I anticipated. At times

I ended up grappling with strange things that appeared that I didn't expect.

I still struggle with this connection between the printed page and reality. I turn to my favorite verses in the Bible, and I read them again and again, daring myself to make them a part of my life, to live out what I read. Wanting to believe the promises of words on a page. Wondering what the fruits of these words might be if I take the next step of faith, if I let them take root. Anticipating the unexpected things that might result.

Over time I got older, and my interests moved more toward boys, less toward growing things. My parents sold the house in the suburbs and moved out to the woods, where my mother could indulge her love for wildflowers and birds.

Recently I drove by the split-level ranch of my childhood. It was almost unrecognizable. In a frenzy of minimalist landscaping, the new young owners had cut everything to the ground and decorated their yard with a few self-conscious junipers and arborvitae, some scarlet geraniums and white petunias.

No children will ever find hiding places in this yard. But maybe, someday, one will beg a little plot in the corner for a garden.

STARRY, STARRY NIGHT

Seeing God in the Bigger Picture

Where do we come from? What are we?
Where are we going?

TITLE OF A PAINTING BY PAUL GAUGUIN

Something cold and wet presses against my side. I am swimming, swimming, up through a thick fog of darkness. There is a rhythmic clicking keeping time with the beating of my heart.

My eyes slide open. One A.M. glows in red neon from the alarm clock on the dresser across the room. Moonlight streams in, casting shadows in dark relief on the floors and walls. The oriental rug is slatted with black bars from the blinds across the windows.

The coldness again. Brown eyes peer hopefully over the comforter. Whenever there is a full moon, our collie is restless. When we first turned off the lights, she lay on the floor at the foot of our bed, chin on paws, sighing deeply from time to time. Through the twilight of first sleep, I was vaguely aware of her restlessness, her toenails tap-tap-tapping as she paced the fifteen-foot length of our wood floor, punctuating my dreams.

I turn my back to her, wrap myself in the covers, but the inevitable comes. A long, wet nose nudges me through my cocoon. A tongue tentatively roughs my cheek. I sigh and swing my feet to the floor, careful not to awaken Jeff, who has to rise early for work.

Joyfully, tail wagging, the dog bounds down the eight steps to the kitchen. I follow her slowly, groping my way through a haze of semiconsciousness, and pad across the cool tile floor. I open the door to the patio, and we both step out into the night.

Or is it night? The moon illuminates my small backyard, its glow throwing oaks and elms into dark silhouettes, their shadows lying in sharp-edged pools upon the lawn.

So bright, this night. I step onto the grass. The humidity of the day is gone, condensed into tiny droplets that gently wash and tickle my bare feet.

The shadows disappear briefly as clouds slide in and out around the moon. The fierce pinpricks of my favorite constellations play hide-and-seek behind the hazy curtain. I scan the horizon for the first glimpse of Orion the Hunter, but he remains below my sight, forestalling the bittersweet announcement of the autumn to come.

Like a stripper shedding her clothes, the moon slips off her clouds and floats through space, revealed in all her cold, hard nakedness.

"Cold hearted orb that rules the night, removes the colours from our sight. Red is grey and yellow white. . . . "©

There is something eternally fascinating about the moon— something primeval in its light, hypnotic in its rhythms. Tides beat a steady time to its insistent cycle. Women's bodies are inexplicably linked with it in a crazy dance. Moonshine for sure. In psych wards, patients are restless when the moon waxes to its full splendor.

Harvest moon. Blue moon. Crescent moon.

Joseph Conrad writes, "There is something haunting in the light of the moon; it has all the dispassionateness of a disembodied soul, and something of its inconceivable mystery."

The crickets thread the warp and the woof of the night with their reverberation, humming and thrumming. A dog barks far away, adding a muffled voice to the design in progress. My dog listens intently to the sound, then goes back to addressing the business at hand.

A splash from the small pond at the foot of the patio adds its own percussion to the night's symphony. A toad, startled by my nearness, seeks watery refuge from the unknown threat I represent, starkly illuminated against the starlit night. He sends ripples across the mat of duckweed floating on the surface, a mosaic of black on the mirror of the water. The moon's reflected whiteness wavers, broken by the spikes of sweet yellow iris and arrowhead knifing their way up through the shallows.

Clouds wisp over the moon, then swirl away. The vast expanse of the universe spreads out like powdered sugar on black velvet.

The roof of the world.

I feel awe yet incalculable loneliness at this glittering heavenly vault, this endless space. I shiver.

Desert mystic Carlo Carretto must have also felt this loneliness as he gazed at the stars in wonder:

Inaccessible far-away things question us endlessly, oblige us to look up at those luminous specks like starry holes piercing the black vault, which seem to say that there, above, is the repose we seek. . . .

How often, lying wrapped in a blanket on the sand, have I passed hour after hour gazing at a starry dome ceaselessly speaking to me, questioning me, helping me to find my bearings in the dark?

Why do we live?

Why do things come to be! . . .

Why this vast silence?

Why do the stars look down as though indifferent to our suffering?

Withal, one thing is certain: this light, the sign of the truth we seek and the means by which we may catch a glimpse of it, has not got its roots on earth.

Light comes from up there, it comes from something stretching above me, something transcending me, something preceding me. . . .

The mystery is there and I cannot escape it. The mystery is there and I cannot avoid it. The mystery is there and I cannot laugh it off.

I know a man who makes a living painting stars and celestial objects for a planetarium. He has always had a passion for creation, but the death of a much-loved grandmother sparked a deep anger in him. He washed his hands of his faith. He turned to science. But science left him empty.

An elderly astronomer spent evenings under the stars with him, letting him talk out his anger. Slowly, my friend found his faith again—but a different type of faith, one that let him embrace sorrow, anger, and suffering, yet find peace and order in the cosmic blueprint of space.

Author Bret Lott took his wife and two young boys out West for the first time. After a long day's travel, they stopped to eat dinner in a roadside café. It was long past sunset when they emerged, carrying their sleepy sons to the car. Overhead was a vast ceiling of stars—harsh, intense, icy-blue stars that in the night sky of their home back East were only faded blurs. Their three-year-old son began crying—terrified at the endless universe that before had been faded and softened—and begged to go back inside.

Star light, star bright, first star I've seen tonight. I wish I may, I wish I might . . .

How insignificant we feel in the face of this black bowl we call night, lit up with sparks kindled from God's own hands!

When I was a child, the night was my friend. Long after sundown, my family slumbering unawares, I would slip outside. Ten steps, then I was clambering up the sweating air-conditioning unit by our toolshed. A quick chin-up, and I was on the roof.

Flat on my back, cotton pajamas pressed into shingles still warm from the day's heat, I would peer through my cheap binoculars and wonder. The Big Dipper was familiar; other constellations were a mystery to me. Yet, although their identities were unknown, I could pick out groupings by sight. Through the randomness of billions of galaxies, my childlike, untrained eyes could still see that there was order and meaning to the arrangements.

So many events in my life now seem odd, random, haphazard. I want quick answers. I want to know now, God, why this is happening. Tell me there is order.

31

I think of my sister's firstborn, missing from birth a slim cord in his brain, which means he will forever struggle in a world that moves too fast for him, that's too loud. My mother's body, ravaged by breast cancer, will never be the same. I remember my college classmate, who chose to delay her chemotherapy in the face of leukemia to birth her baby daughter, then died an early death. Teresa of Avila said it best: "God, if this is how you treat your friends, no wonder you have so few of them!"

Timothy Ferris observes in *The Whole Shebang*, "Human beings must be just about the loneliest species in the universe. We've only recently begun to learn about the universe, don't know yet quite what to make of it . . . so we talk among ourselves, in musings that necessarily are limited to our necessarily human perspective."

Lonely, yes. Carl Sagan muses, "Who are we? We find that we live on an insignificant planet of a humdrum star lost in a galaxy tucked away in some forgotten corner of the universe in which there are far more galaxies than people."

Forgotten? Are we? Has God turned his eyes to another galaxy? Another planet far away? Has he despaired of us? Have we despaired of him?

"When I consider your heavens, the work of your fingers, the moon and the stars, which you have set in place, what is man that you are mindful of him, the son of man that you care for him?"

I call the dog, softly, adding another sound to the night's sonata.

32

Are our lives like the night sky? Is all the apparent randomness that happens to us really a fast-turning wheel of divine order?

In his book, *Arctic Dreams*, Barry Lopez sees the structure in the natural world and desires it for himself: "I wish the order of my life to be arranged in the same way I find the light, the slight movement of the wind, the voice of a bird, the heading of a seed pod I see before me. This impeccable and indisputable integrity I want in myself."

In the Chicago suburb where I live, light pollution is an ever present distraction. It's only late at night that my gaze can penetrate the orange haze in the sky to really see the stars. I wrap myself in an afghan and wait. As the hour grows later, lights are turned off all around the city and the night sky comes into focus like a print in a developing tray. First Jupiter, a fiery glow in the west. Cassiopeia's tilted jagged "W" is next in the north, then I spot the Big Dipper. I look straight up and make out the Northern Cross blinking into life at the sky's zenith.

How old are the stars? Some scientists hypothesize that they may be fourteen billion years old. Many of the stars I am looking at are long dead, exploded. They died a fiery death; their light is but a bright shadow finishing a haunted journey started years before my birth.

I know there are other stars I cannot see. Newly formed, their light has not yet crossed the black chasm of space to reach my eyes.

33

The world I know on a daily basis is but a stop on the journey. So much seen, so much unseen and yet to come. I stand trembling on the porch, lost under the constellations wheeling over my head.

Wrapping my arms around my chest, hugging myself, I call the dog again. Together we step back into the familiar darkness of the house.

Pond Musings

Signs of Life, Signs of Change

All changes, even the most longed for, have
their melancholy, for what we leave behind
us is a part of ourselves; we must die to one
life before we can enter into another.

ANATOLE FRANCE

There is something fascinating about water. I'm drawn to ponds in the woods, the reflections of trees on the surface of puddles in the road, the sun sparkling on a creek's fluid rapids. The sound of water moving is a siren's song calling me to come closer, to listen to the thunky, hollow splashes of toads and spring peepers as they christen themselves in watery depths. I love to trail my hand through the wetness and peel off my socks and shoes and wade into it.

In *The Magician's Nephew*, a volume in the Chronicles of Narnia series, children make their way out of the chaotic, worry-filled place in which they live by slipping on magic rings. They arrive at a world-between-worlds, dotted with ponds. By choosing a pool of water and slipping into it, they can make their way to another place, a place that beckons, that excites, that is unknown. New worlds to explore.

I want this magic for myself. I will make a pond.

Digging anywhere in the Chicago suburbs is an undertaking not to be underestimated. Before your shovel can lift dirt, you need to call JULIE. No, not a girl. JULIE is a company that controls the labyrinth of cables and cords that runs throughout subdivisions, bearing gifts of electricity, gas, telephone service, and cable television. Upon phoning JULIE, an alarm call is dispatched to all utilities: "This woman is going to dig!" Within forty-eight hours, trucks descend on our driveway, bringing men in jumpsuits with their names emblazoned on the pockets and a truckload of marking equipment to outline their cables. Fluorescent orange flags. Spray paint. Yellow tags and ribbons.

By the time they finish, our already rather ugly backyard is a cross between a fluorescent orange spider web and a miniature golf course.

Despite the maze of flags and spray paint, I manage to find a spot by the patio that is miraculously unmarked by utility lines. With determination, I outline a seven-by-ten-foot spot below the grassy slope at the bottom of the patio steps and break ground. No champagne christening or ribbons on the shovels. I chug down a Diet Coke in honor of the occasion.

A ragged, cavernous hole takes shape. It looks as if a wayward meteorite blasted into the side of the patio. A gaping, sullen hole.

Jeff comes home for dinner and surveys my handiwork. I babble nervously about the virtues of a pond, the value of attracting wildlife, the beauty of water in the landscape.

"Aha," he says. He looks pensive. He loves me. "Whatever you want to do. . . ."

A week passes. Rain falls with depressing frequency. The dirt I've excavated from the yawning hole is a slush pile on the patio. I never thought about what to do with the leftover dirt when I started this project. And now it's mud. Where do I put all this muddy clay in our small backyard? And why didn't I shift it before the monsoons moved in?

My garden books are no help—none of them offer advice on what action to take if you have a torrential downpour in the middle of your pond excavation. The hole I've dug is full of water. I now have a very good idea of what my finished pond is going to look like; I also have a pretty good feel for how much clay and hardpan is in our backyard. The water is lapping over the top of the pit and shows no signs of draining. I still haven't gotten the money for a liner, and the thought of bailing out all that water is as appealing as sitting through a Johnny Mathis concert.

Uncle. I'm ready to call it quits.

New and pressing problems develop with each passing day. A nearby resident mentions a city ordinance that says yards with "water features" must be fenced. In frustration, I throw a plastic tarp over the sodden chasm.

Other neighbors casually drop by and inquire about our activities. Are we having sewer problems? No, I tell them. We're adding a pond. "Oh," they say, eyebrows arching, unspoken thoughts in cartoon balloons over their heads. "How nice."

That's it. I'm going to fill it in. Tomorrow. I'll have a fine, double-dug flower bed by the patio. No more pond. I pull up the tarp, roll it, and set it aside. Water is still lapping over the edges of the hole. Tomorrow, I promise myself. Jeff looks relieved when I tell him.

Coming back after lunch out the next day, we find a pair of mallards casing the backyard in the wet drizzle—literally, a day for ducks. My twelve-year-old daughter, Jenny, immediately christens them Fred and Freda. The mallard and his mate spot the pond in progress and go in for a short dip.

I'm bounding all over the room. I'm jumping up and down. Ducks! Wildlife! Here in our suburban yard, because of our pond. Jeff looks resigned. I go out and begin carting the dirt to the back of the shed with our rusty wheelbarrow before I change my mind about the whole thing.

Pausing to rest, I survey the situation. The pond is ugly. The ragged edges of the concrete patio show like the frayed edge of a rubbled cloth against the cloudy water. Algae is beginning to bloom as a chartreuse scum on the surface. I need a plan.

Plan A: the formal pond. The pond books all contain a laundry list of the hardware and software you need if you are going to add a pond to your landscape. Pumps. Liners. Filters. More pumps. Drains. Boulders. More pumps. Chemicals. Tubes. Decorative lighting. Waterfall pumps.

I price these at Home Depot. I look at the checkbook balance. I mentally run the figures again. Doing things the natural way is looking attractive. On to plan B.

Plan B: the natural pond. I decide to use the existing clay-based earth as my liner. God doesn't use a plastic liner, does he? And his ponds look great. Natural is good. Natural is the way to go. Natural fits my bank account. Natural is cheap. Cheap is good.

I try to "think natural" as I watch the pond over the next few weeks. The spinachy scum takes on a life of its own. The life cycle of a "natural" pond includes algae bloom in the spring.

In dismay, I watch my small pool turn from brown to lime then back again, a rotating whirligig of botanical affliction. Visitors to my backyard are polite but skeptical. What exactly am I trying to do here, anyway, I ask myself? A fetid smell wafts from the pond. I get a whiff. I need professional help.

A friend who makes his living doing landscape restoration offers advice and solace. There are too many nutrients washing down the hill into the water, he observes. Try plants. They'll soak up some of the runoff.

Off to the plant nursery. In giant metal bathtubs soak the plants I envision bringing my backyard ecology experiment into amicable balance. Sweet yellow flag. Siberian iris. Japanese iris. Single and double flowering arrowheads—I can't choose between them. "When in doubt, buy both" is my gardening philosophy. Eden is just around the corner.

I place my new plants into the pond and wait for a miracle. Instead, I get more algae bloom. The green stuff is beginning to prey on my mind, color my dreams. I try to divert myself with a morning cup of coffee and the newspaper. As I read, an article on harnessing pond scum as a potential energy source jumps out at me. I mull it over, thinking it sounds appealing, then realize it's time to take drastic measures.

I consider my options. Cash is beginning to be a problem. Ecological balance doesn't come without a price, I remind myself—and look at all the money I saved by not buying the liners and pumps! But a virtual snake is lurking in my Eden, although no real ones have taken up residence yet in the pond. The algae blooms again. Perhaps, suggests my water gardening book, goldfish will help.

Off to the pet store. A wall of glassed-in oceans beckons. At the very bottom of the food chain, under the pricey saltwater glamour fish, is a large murky tank of Comet goldfish—a bargain at fourteen cents each. I take twenty-five, rationalizing that most of them won't make it and that I am saving them from the fate of being feeder fish for, say, a piranha, or some other flesh-eating aquatic species.

Jenny and I float the plastic Glad bag of assorted fish on the murky pool, and after acclimating the fish to the temperature of their new home, we release them from their plastic prison. They immediately disappear into the swampy shallows. *Now we see through a glass darkly* . . . We try to see them in vain. After watching for a while, we return to the house.

Over the course of the next weeks, Jenny brings me a daily corpse count as one by one the goldfish go belly-up. From twenty-five to ten in two weeks. The floaters line the grassy banks, bloated, white-stomached. I skim them off the surface and put them in the compost pile, close to where we buried our two pet rabbits. *From dust thou came, to dust thou wilt return* (though I'm not sure if this applies to fish).

The water level is holding pretty steady, thanks to the blue clay layer of earth I hit about twenty-four inches down. I plant some marsh marigolds, which I hope will fill in the bare spots where the water runs up against the concrete steps. The water clarity is also improving—now it's light greenish black, which is better than neon lime green or opaque brown, and I can see the fish moving around toward the bottom.

I'm adjusting my preconceptions of what this pond will be. One thing I realize is that a natural pond is not like a concrete

41

fountain or a pool with a liner. It will never be clear or ornamental in the way ponds are in glossy magazine garden layouts or the water garden at my local arboretum. I'm wondering if I can get comfortable with this or not—if I can change my expectations.

I experience moments of serendipity amid the frustrations. This watery mud hole is a magnet for creatures I've never seen in our pocket-sized yard before. The butterflies like the mud, and they add their collage of blues, apricots, blacks, and yellows to the earth tones of the pond. The buff-and-cream field sparrows decorate the edges, venturing out on the rocks I dropped in strategic spots along the watery rim. They splash dust from their feathers and cautiously sip microscopic drinks from their pebbled perches. Mud daubers explore the swampy corners. Bring on the snakes and turtles, and we'll have something to brag about.

Algae blooms, then subsides. The pond plants begin to take root. Duckweed comes in, a casual hitchhiker on one of the arrowhead plants. Like a vegetative Mafia, it takes over, matting the surface. Change. Metamorphosis. Mutation. Variation.

Where once was grass and muck is now something in process, something of promise.

I dip my fingers into the pond and trail them through the muddy water. Life is unsure. Change is inevitable. But here is new growth, a fresh start.

INTO THE TUNNEL

Facing the Future with Hope

Now constantly there is the sound, quieter
than rain, of the leaves falling . . . the life of
summer falls silent, and the nights grow.

WENDELL BERRY

Autumn blew in through my open windows last night, delighting in catching me slightly off guard. Its dry, lightly burnt smell was tinged with a crisp anticipation, a foreshadowing of sadness. The first time you breath it in, you know with mingled dread and fascination that the tunnel of darkness is coming, the descent into the newly dug grave of winter. The months of gloom suddenly loom ahead, day gradually losing its battle with the night.

Welcome back, season of slow decline.

In our bedroom, the extra blankets come out although the windows stay open. We sleep deeply, the cool air driving us under layers of covers, hibernation a tantalizing possibility. In the morning, light comes through the curtains, slow and late, making it difficult to break the bonds of unconsciousness. Days shorten. By mid-afternoon, long shadows grip the lawn, and a hint of twilight steals across the sky.

A harvest moon hangs just above the trees in the evening, an unearthly orange globe surely too heavy to make its journey through the heavens. Later, it shines small and cold above me in the night. Orion peeks over the horizon, a hesitant hunter steeling himself to climb the winter firmament.

In the morning, there's a diffusion in the air; everything's a little pixelled, a little grainy. The light slants in a way that you can't quite put your finger on; things look backlit. As I dress, I listen to the radio on which a woman wails, "Everything is temporary . . ." I wonder.

The wind has a slight edge, a coolness that belies the intense heat of the sun, which shines round and burnished in a deep blue dome. The plant world is closing up shop. There's a last gasp of manufacturing seeds, sent aloft via parachute or dropped into soil beneath their stalks. The seeds slip into dormancy, a one-way trip for some, others resurrecting in the spring.

Maybe.

Warblers, impossible to distinguish from one another, exchange migration directions from the branches of bur oaks along the trails I walk. Already, the black walnut trees are disrobing, shedding their pinnate leaves, dropping them like skirts around their ankles. Their trunks and limbs are slim and clean. A few twinned balls of green cling to the branches; others lie cracked and broken under my feet, oozing inky black grease from their rock-like centers.

Debilitated corpses of once vital wildflowers are crumpling into brown crepe paper, crushed by some cosmic fist, their colors sucked back into the earth. They stagger, muted and dead in blacks and grays. Burn victims they are, survivors of a fiery episode, yet the only flame that has touched them is summer sunshine, now disappeared.

The grasses crackle where once they sighed. Dry as death, hollow as an echo, they accept their lot in life. The expiration date is here. Pink slips have been handed out, and they, dignified, make the best of it.

The wardrobe of autumn leans heavily toward ochers, amethysts, rusts, limes. Plants dress themselves for the Day of Reckoning. Bees work the goldenrods for last-minute nectar to store against starvation. Then, they bumble through the asters, which brave the death all around them with their blooms. Willow asters. Sky Blue asters. New England. Smooth.

Butterflies mirror the vegetation's autumn clothes—sulphurs cavort together, monarchs in orange and black strain the sun like stained-glass windows, an occasional cabbage white butterfly dotted with gray alights on a limb. Goldfinches erupt from the prairie floor, donning the colors of the grasses: yellow mixed with olive, tipped in browns and blacks.

Squirrels step up their pace of living, racing from tree to tree, commuters late for the work of storehousing sustenance for winter to come. In my backyard, they clean out the peanut and sunflower seed feeders, then lick the ledge clean of birdseed where once they daintily chose only the best morsels. In moments, they shear off ears of corn nailed to the squirrel feeder by my window, leaving only unclad cobs. Finches mob the seed trays, furiously cracking sunflower kernels in their beaks, storing up fuel for the apocalypse ahead.

A chipmunk scrambles across the path, nut clasped in its jaws, tail stiff and upright like a bicycle flag. A flurry of fur.

Glancing at me in alarm, he brakes, squealing. His paws leave tread marks in the dirt as he doubles back and darts to shelter.

The Indian grass colors have leached away—newly bleached plumes gradating down to lime at their bases. The once green prairie sea has turned pale, striped with dead brown sticks, depleted of sap. I chew on grass stems, once juicy and wet, now woody and stiff.

Satin ruby berries dangle in clusters overhanging the creek, which runs colder in anticipation of the icy entombment to come. In still places, the water reflects the autumn skies, the clouds graphic in patterns I imagine as a frog, an angel, a ship in full sail.

Queen Anne's lace flower heads clench tight in dried skeletal umbrellas. Dragonflies buzz the tallgrass, like moving flints of copper. Grasshoppers clatter like castanets on the path, then take winged flight—temporary butterfly look-alikes. Fiddling while Rome is burning, burning; making merry while the sun shines. The hot buttered popcorn smell of prairie dropseed tickles my nose.

In summer, the soft tallgrass stroked my legs. In its death throes now, it scratches and marks. The silphiums leave my bare legs raw where I brush against their textured leaves. Purple coneflower seed heads are prickly dark satellites, tearing at my clothes; rattlesnake master's spiny globes cat-claw my arms.

A few late gentians are open, blue on blonde grass. Prairie clover has gone to seed, dry cones on stark stalks. Roundheaded bush clover bravely waves brown clusters, scattered

47

pom-pom girls cheering the autumn season to climax. Go, go, go!

New England asters stab the prairie with color, opening fringed dark purple flowers buttoned with golden centers, radiating a slightly piney scent. They cluster at the end of each stalk, small bouquets of living color against a dying landscape. A froth of heath asters throws itself across the path, foaming at the stem, oblivious to winter's destruction just around the bend. Cup plant torches are burnt out tapers, leaves wrinkled and dead. Beads of rosin on a compass plant's broken stem glisten, immobilized, crystallized. Indian plantain's hard green seed heads fluff out, flattened tops lifted shoulder-high across the prairie, sending embryos of new life across the grassy plain, ensuring survival if winter does indeed end. Their leaves wrap closer to the main stems, folding themselves in a protective embrace, a last-ditch effort to ward off the grim reaper lying in wait.

The wind undulates across the prairie. There is a whisper of desperation in its sound, a sigh of depression. The darkness is coming. The world is dying. A mammoth meltdown, colors draining, the equinox clock ticking toward dormancy. A chain saw buzzes in the distance. More death. The smell of decomposition laces the atmosphere. The killing fields are as close as the first frost.

The seasons cycle. Repeat refrain. The same four choruses, sung over and over again. Yet even as autumn is upon me, I wonder if this time it will be different. If the final stanza will be sung, the snows will stay, and spring will never come. The needle stuck on the phonograph, unending. Will Aslan breathe his warm breath on the earth and crack the ice again? Or will the darkness win over the light? I want to believe. I do believe. God, help me believe.

Dead leaves crunch under my feet as I walk and question. The merry-go-round spins faster, accelerates. I am helpless, along for the ride of the seasonal cycle over which I have no control. I can only close my eyes, accepting the journey, hoping that spring will come.

A TALE
OF THREE GARDENS

Lessons Learned
in Developing a Personal Faith

A permanent state of transition is man's most noble condition.

JUAN RAMON JIMENEZ

50

My yard lies at the intersection of two conflicting philosophies of gardening, a virtual neutral zone between the Hatfields and McCoys.

In this corner, meet Gerry. Gerry approaches his lawn with the exuberant passion of a naturalist. Native plants only, please. No aliens need apply. He dispenses Latin names like my kids' Pez units dispense pastel candy pellets. *Solidago. Silphium. Andropogon gerardii.* Prime his verbal pump, and he'll spout phrases like "our mother earth" and "plants must be allowed to reproduce and birth children." Gerry has written books thicker than Chicago's metro telephone directory about plants and tramped over every inch of land in DuPage County.

Wood chip paths meander through a yard that screams neglect to the uninitiated. Tall goldenrod, clumps of wine-colored big bluestem, and sprays of hairy asters all mesh together amid a tangle of upstart seedlings from nearby trees. When Gerry set fire to his yard this fall "as part of nature's natural cycle," my neighbor two doors down was hysterical. "Too lazy to mow" was her emphatic verdict as she dialed the police.

And in this corner is Jim. A disciple of the American suburban yard ethos, he is lauded by the neighborhood as the ideal retired gentleman gardener. Each summer, the sounds of his Briggs & Stratton mower drift across the fence with the regularity of a senior citizen who drinks a glass of prune juice every day. He adheres to the "square-foot gardening method"— everything in rectangular raised beds fashioned by four-by-fours—and carefully lines his side of the fence with metal sheeting to keep his black, fertile soil from washing into my yard, which is on the downhill slope from his.

Sugar snap peas in orderly regiments troop up his trellises. Creamy banana peppers, unmarred clutches of Blue Lake green beans, and cascades of Celebrity tomatoes gush forth from Jim's garden. The harvest is so abundant that we often find pans of produce left for us on the back porch during the peak season—a bountiful suburban potlatch.

An ample dressing of mushroom farm compost and some quick squirts of state-of-the-art chemicals ensure that no neighbor of Jim goes wanting for veggies during Chicago's gardening season.

Jim attacks his yard with an arsenal of weaponry. His chipper/shredder, tiller, sprayer, mower, and chain saw make an appearance whenever a stray branch or leaf threatens the smooth expanse of lawn and geometrical precision of shrubs and trees. He boasts the world's sturdiest wheelbarrow, and his compost is made in an immense green plastic drum the size of an industrial concrete mixer. Home Depot dearly loves Jim.

The two gardens run like watercolors down the hillside and mix in the palette of my backyard, the blended child of diverse but talented parents. Where Jim's brush touches, squared brick boxes of herbs stand in neat order by my patio. Gerry's paint spills over in the wildness of my small pond and my drifts of big bluestem. My canvas includes coneflowers and cauliflower. Tallgrass and tomatoes. Indian grass and iris. Prim hybrid roses rub shoulders with primitive rattlesnake master waving its threatening head in disorderly chaos.

Unpredictable things happen. I turn my back, and my water-loving arrowheads wander from the pond out into the marshy yard, poking up in the thick of the tame subdivision lawn grass. While I sleep, insurgent sunflowers take root behind the glamour-girl roses and send up stalks six feet tall. Within this overflow of unplanned infiltration, I stumble over strangers who have made themselves at home in my herb garden. I trip over tangles of tree saplings tarrying in my tomato beds.

Poet Jane Kenyon felt this tension: "The balance of power in a garden is never the same from year to year. You never grow the same garden twice, try as you may. . . . It is troubling to decide what shall live and what shall die."

Troubling indeed. Weed identification book in hand, I often lie in the grass in my backyard, mulling over which uninvited guests must be chucked out, which endured, and which welcomed as a delightful diversion. Each decision I make will have a long-term effect. I prune back branches that wander, shading some of my desirable plants. A snip here, a cut there . . . a semblance of order.

Growth is often dictated by neglect rather than serendipity. Occasionally, I let something go and get more than I bargained for. Some of these aliens I admire at first, then belatedly find they are noxious weeds in beautiful disguises. At first I admire the Canada thistle, whose purple powder puffs atop pineapple-patterned cups are so exquisitely intriguing. Reading up on it, I see that its terrifyingly deep roots will hinder other plants from growing properly. When I recognize it as an intruder bent on destruction, I ruthlessly rip it out.

Mulberry saplings are birthed by a neighbor's tree and work their way into the landscape almost overnight. Sternly, I institute a border patrol around the rim of my yard. Immigration quotas are imposed.

Other unfamiliar specimens I learn to accept and enjoy, letting them become a piece in my garden puzzle, a part of the picture, a color in the ever widening palette I use. I allow some of my wild sunflowers to take root and grow behind the roses, their shaggy yellow heads a foil to the hot pinks and vivid reds. I let the lime green sedges roam through my prairie spot, bristly seed tops contrasting with the soft rounded ovals of lead plant's leafy foliage. The golden dandelions live in harmony with my bluegrass lawn. Daisy fleabane wanders over from another yard, and its tiny white inflorescences are a backdrop for the pink blooms of my butterfly weed.

Wild or docile. Rampant or restrained. As with my garden, I feel myself tugged first in one direction then another in my beliefs. My faith was once more structured. Like Jim's garden, everything was painstakingly planned. I accepted the faith of my childhood, swallowed it whole. Every doctrine I was taught was correct to the last jot and tittle, every piece of information mortared in as solidly as the bricks in my planter boxes. My childhood faith was like my first gardens: meticulous, boxed in with wooden two-by-fours, the dirt sifted for rocks, every seed dropped into a measured-out hole.

This solid framework is still there, the underpinnings in place, sturdy as a fortress. As my author friend Robert Benson says, it gives me "something to nail to." The boxes are full of rich black soil from years of maintenance and care. Yet, unfamiliar things are spilling over the framework, drifting down the hillside, mingling with the things I know well. Challenging questions cause some previously trained shrubs to sprawl wildly, stab up a surprised shoot here, send out an imprudent limb there. Strange substances ramble through the demureness.

I immerse myself in reading and look up to find something blooming that I hadn't planted. I mull over a conversation with a friend, and branches begin leafing out in bizarre places. Someone I love develops an incurable illness, and curious creepers come out and twine around my trellises. I'm questioning, thinking, asking, "Why?"

A part of me longs for inflexible order, the decisiveness of framed boxes. It's so much easier to pull up everything that slips out-of-bounds than to take time to examine each new element and figure out if it fits or if it fractures the whole. Another part of me wants to let everything run wild. Close my eyes. Accept it all.

I'm trying to make sense of things, trying to find balance. Trying not to lose my unshakable framework, but also trying not to fear loosening up a little bit, letting the garden be a bit wilder, appreciating what might seem out of control for the moment but being wise enough to cut back that which would wreak havoc and destroy the beauty of the whole.

This tension, this pull. A stretching that keeps me constantly on tenterhooks, wondering what's next, what's coming around the bend.

Theologian Walter Brueggemann found that "a sense of place is a primary category of faith." Despite the uncertainty of my shifting landscape, I feel joy. In this melting pot of my backyard and my faith, I am finding a sense of peace, a sense of place.

6

On Pruning

Getting Rid of Excess Baggage
Will Make You Stronger

It is not what you are nor what you have been
that God sees with his all-merciful eyes, but
what you desire to be.

WILLIAM JOHNSTON

Caught in the tangle of covers on my bed, I stare at the moon-light shaping shadows on the wall. Thoughts unwind in my head like a ball of yarn unraveling. Meaningless, meaningless, all seems meaningless. A motion picture plays in my mind of events that seem senseless, hurtful.

The wasteland of the soul is where I wander, and there is no compass in my hand. Arctic winds howl; I am chilled to the bone. No stars illuminate the night; no porch light is on to guide me home.

I fall into a half sleep—restless, lightly dreaming. My mind wanders to images of my long-ago orchard. Scenes flash through my thoughts.

It's a hazy November evening, and I am perched in the crotch of a neglected, ancient Jonathan apple tree, precariously balanced in my worn-out Reeboks. Reaching for a limb, I wield the sharpened pruning tool. Unproductive branches fall like rain around the aged tree. Errant boughs that had meandered into the open center are ruthlessly pared away with my razor-edged tool.

A homely, sunburned man taught me the art of pruning, showed me the way of the saw. He promised that the hoary tree would fruit again if I freed her from her excess branches.

Could it be true?

Killing the old to bring forth the new. The dead wood drops, disconnected. The water sprouts in profuse disharmony are deliberately cut away. Next are the suckers that have shot up at the base of the gnarled tree, parasitic, sapping its life away in bits and pieces.

A careless move—my hand is nicked. A line of crimson streaks my palm.

This is my blood . . . which is poured out for many. . . .

I suck the spot, tasting the saltiness of blood and skin. I think of sacrifice.

The saw flashes again. The tree is emerging, cleaner, lighter, raising her arms in newfound lightness to the sky.

In her book *A Hundred White Daffodils*, Jane Kenyon pruned the trees that overhung her garden: "It's not just more flowers I want, it's more light, more air for flowers, more sun for cheerfulness. A person gets her fill of shade-loving plants."

I've had my fill of darkness. But there is so much to prune away. So many extra branches, so much excess baggage. Worry. Anxiety. Selfishness. Old grievances unforgiven. Hurts from my childhood. Guilt over past actions. Bad decisions I've made. They draw energy from me, sucking my strength, siphoning away my stamina for living.

I long for light.

I lop off more apple branches.

It's not enough to haphazardly cut the tree. Each cut has to be carefully evaluated, each wound intentionally inflicted for good. A wrong cut, and I might set the tree back for years.

Still in my half-dreaming wakefulness, I remember other trees, other yards. I see their faded images like tintypes in my memory. I remember one of my favorites, in the yard of an old house, with a beautiful woods.

We first saw the house in a classified ad, and I immediately took my red pen and circled the description. We were looking for a place with some trees, a house with some space for our growing family. I wanted room to expand my garden, which had threatened to take over every nook and cranny of our cramped yard. The realtor drove us up the driveway of the thirty-year-old ranch house with three acres, shown in black and white in the computer printout she provided. Feeling like Dorothy stepping from the drab Kansas farmhouse into Oz, I saw the monochromatic image in my hand turn to a dazzling display of color as we parked the car and stepped out by the "For Sale" sign.

A crab apple bloomed in burgundy explosions; the grass spread in emerald hues against a backdrop of ancient white and gray sycamores. The centerpiece of the front yard was two twenty-five-year-old Bradford pear trees, each one a poster child for the species. *I think that I shall never see . . .* The trees welcomed me. I had no eyes for the house, only the trees. And these two were just the beginning. There were acres of trees, a diversity of trees, an abundance of trees, a plethora of trees. Catalpa. Sugar maple. Dogwood. Redbud. Persimmon.

One look. I was hooked. Easiest sale the realtor ever made.

The two pear trees were the crowning glory of the property and the delight of my heart. The trees' vase-shaped limbs were vested in snowy blooms each spring, torches of crimson foliage in fall. No sweet smell to their blooms, but the subtle odor of pollen and the sound of buzzing bees visiting each flower.

Our children and their friends loved to hang from the upper branches in the spring, hidden from view, then drop like acorns to terrorize the unwary. When I mowed the light covering of bluegrass and moss under each tree in the summer, circling Zen-like ever wider around the trunks, I loved to brush against the trees' shiny kelly-green leaves. In the winter, the snows penciled in alabaster threads of pearl outlining their well-shaped limbs, drifting in whitecaps around their sable trunks. Our December landscape, full of blackened tree candles stuck haphazardly in the snowbanks, resembled a vanilla-frosted birthday cake.

Our trees looked strong, invincible. I basked in the security of their branches.

Then came the storm.

I remember how the window blinds lifted one night, almost torn from their screw holds by the violence of the wind, waking us from a sound sleep. We heard a mighty crash. For a moment the wind was silent, then a howling, haunting chorus arose again. I pushed the blinds aside and peered out into the darkness, my face pressed against the window. All I saw was blackness. I uneasily returned to bed and snuggled closer to Jeff, wrapping my arms around his back.

Sun shone through the battered blinds at 6:00 A.M. that long-ago morning, bringing me groggily back to consciousness. I stretched and tentatively slipped out of bed. Remembering the crash of the night before, I opened the blinds and stared out in disbelief.

One Bradford pear tree lay mutilated across the grass, its uppermost branches barely skimming our bedroom walls. Its rain-soaked trunk was black with water, its leaves spangled with a thousand raindrop prisms. Jagged edges of the trunk rose into the air. A bird's nest, broken, was strewn crazily across the scene.

Later, the sound of our friend's chain saw tore through me, ripping my heart as the branches of the tree were carved into fireplace-sized pieces for the winter. Despondent, grieving, I hooked up my large hauler to the riding lawn mower and began moving the larger logs to the wood rick. My nine-year-old son, Dustin, followed me, trundling twigs in his red Flyer wagon. I hardened my heart against the loss.

My tree. My tree.

Glorious on the outside, our beautiful tree had decayed inside. We never suspected anything was amiss beneath its bark. Stressed by the storm, splintered and broken, the tree revealed its rot.

The original planters of the tree had pruned it to a vase shape, which left a hollow between the three main branches that diverged from the main trunk. Rainwater would sit, cupped between the branches, dissolving the tender bark, rotting the tree from within. The decision made long ago to prune the branches in that manner had been a disastrous one—with consequences that weren't evident until the tree was under stress.

In what ways am I pruning my own life?

I'm still half asleep, considering. I think again of my apple orchard. I remember how the experience with the rotten

Bradford pear tree helped me when I pruned my apple trees, how I worked carefully in light of my remembrances. I close my eyes and consider how to prune, thinking of the future rather than the present. I make another cut; another branch falls. Yet, although I'm severing shrewdly, I must also be bold. Most gardeners err on the side of caution when pruning rather than taking out all the excess that needs to be removed. This boldness is learned mostly through experience rather than from books and advice. The outcome of a hard pruning is bountiful results—and gives the gardener courage to cut more next time, to tackle the big branches as well as the small.

I'm feeling courageous. More branches fall.

I dream of the snow-white smoke of apple blossoms in April, a forerunner of a renewed harvest to come. Bees will find my tree again. Sipping nectar, they will add her apple perfume to their golden honey and bless the blooms with possibilities.

My daughter will swing on the cast-off tire I will tie with a sturdy rope to the thickest limb of the soon-vibrant, strong-branched tree. Within its renewed vigor, she will find safety and security, new confidence in herself.

My son's eager fingers will pick the globes of crunchy, slightly tart fruit, and he will toss the cores into the woods as he plays. New trees will spring up from the seeds that bury themselves in the leafy mold.

I smell the hot scent of the applesauce I will can in September. I see the sterilized mason jars clouded by steam, lined up on the kitchen countertop to receive the harvest—a harvest impossible without killing off part of my tree, impossible without loss, without pain. Jane Kenyon expresses this: "Little deaths. Somewhere in the psyche all these changes and losses register as death. What shall we do against it? One might bake a pie. . . . 'Comfort me with apples.' . . . It is a fine thing to build a pie, a bulwark against autumnal entropy."

In Grandmother's antique pie dish I will fill a floury pie crust with apples born of my pruning, crafting a woven lattice across the top, sprinkled with sugar. This will be my legacy, gifts to feed my family.

From the "little deaths" will come strength, growth. The cuts will yield good fruit, new creativity.

In my dreams, the tree trembles from my cutting, but the wind is still. Despite the chill, I am sweating. The hours pass. Darkness falls. It is then I see my hands, my blistered fingers, the palms crisscrossed with a myriad of tiny cuts.

I slide down the rough trunk and flex painfully. Tipping my head to look at the tree, Jupiter winks back at me, the first evening star caught in its branches. Stark black limbs pierce the crystal-cold winter night, their members amputated and strewn around the trunk—a tree holocaust.

Vulnerable, naked against the starlight, my tree looks unable to withstand the winter yet to come.

I have done all I can. Spring will tell if the cuts will heal, if the scars will be buried in blossoms.

COUNTRY GIRL, CITY LIFE

Finding Peace through Acceptance

Be patient toward all that is unsolved in your heart and try to love the questions them-selves. . . . Perhaps you will . . . gradually, without noticing it, live along some distant day into the answer.

RAINER MARIA RILKE

My garden is my healing place, a hospital ward for nursing my wounded spirit. Whenever we move and land in unfamiliar territory, the first thing I do is put growing things into the earth of my new yard. My refuge is then in place, a retreat in time of disruption.

Today, I'm planting herbs. I inhale the scents of thyme, basil, oregano. I caress the texture of the leaves with my fingertips. Some leaves are fuzzy and soft, others silky and shiny. I drink in the colors—multiple shades of green, ranging from blue-green to olive to lime. A chlorophyll kaleidoscope paradise.

I breathe the pungent smell of damp earth. I luxuriate in the slick-wet feel of it between my hands as I press the dirt around the small plants. My herbs won't like it here at first in the hardpan clay of the Chicago suburbs. They desire well-drained, sandy soil. Life isn't always a bed of roses, I tell them. Life is what you make it. Get used to it.

As a gardener, I know it is important that I not be overly gentle with these seedlings. With care, I vigorously pull the root ball of the lemon thyme apart, jam it into a muddy hole filled with water, then firmly pack the earth around the roots. I make sure no air holes are left that might cause the roots to rot and that the roots come into contact firmly with the soil. Once the earth is in place, I snip off leaves until the plant appears scraggly and forlorn, knowing the roots will be better able to support a few leaves on top than a complete plant.

Living in the city, even one as suburban as Glen Ellyn, requires a radical shift in my thinking and focus. I have always believed that morally, physically, and spiritually, it is somehow better to live rurally—to raise children in the country. Early in our marriage, I was enamored with a story in *Mother Earth News* that showed in glowing four-color photo spreads the glories of living in the wilderness of British Columbia. I tried to convince Jeff that somehow God was calling us to move there, an area accessible only by helicopter and canoe. There we would live off the land—raise chickens and goats, tend organic vegetables, homeschool our two children, and chop our own firewood. My husband, who is very talented but whose tool belt—if he had one—would consist of a hammer and a screwdriver, said simply "Honey, you married the wrong man for this!"

Marriage is about compromise. We stayed put.

God has an infinite sense of humor and unfailing knowledge of what is best for us. I've moved from three acres in Indiana, to an acre in Tennessee, to this pocket handkerchief of a yard in suburban Chicago. What is God up to anyway? What about *my* ideas for my life, my children's lives?

67

Years later, when I read about the dissolution of the marriage of the two Canadian homesteaders and their disillusionment with finding happiness together in the wild, it should have been a clue. Maybe, just maybe what I went looking for was in my own backyard. Rather than finding happiness in three hundred acres of Canadian wilderness, with all the moral virtue this implied, perhaps it could be found right here, right now, in suburban Chicago. There's no place like home. There's no place like home. Could this be home?

Oh, God, I miss the stars though. The light pollution in the eastern sky allows only glimpses of my old favorites, often muffled and blurred behind a dirty haze. When I feel a surge of sadness over constellations lost, I pay attention to the bits of beauty around me. With practice, I'm learning to concentrate on what is healing and glorious rather than what is destructive and ugly about the city. I'm seeing the little things rather than looking at the "big picture" of nature, bringing small pieces of it into focus.

Artist Georgia O'Keeffe observed, "When you see a flower, up close, it becomes your whole world for the moment." She learned as a child that sometimes beauty is best seen in the microcosm rather than the macrocosm.

Georgia was right. Beauty doesn't have to be a panoramic view of the mountains. It's the whitewashed bloodroot, opening its shell-white petals in my wildflower garden, powdery saffron stamens stretching toward the sunshine. The raspy, toothed leaves of rattlesnake master poking up through last year's oak leaves on a spring morning in my prairie plot. The flash of chrome sparked by sunlight as Comet goldfish dart through my tiny pond. A symphony of rosy house finches that carry on a conversation from the feeder as I read my book on the back porch. The rangy sunflowers that spring up unbidden, heirs of the snacks the squirrels drop. With their numerically correct swirls of seeds, the heavy-headed sunflowers are rough dinner plates pecked at by the goldfinches that flit in and hang on to their sunny faces, enjoying their sunflower seed supper. God's beauty from odds and ends—the scrap basket of creation.

I admit there is beauty in the big picture here if I patiently look for it. When I cry over the stars I can no longer see in the murky yellow polluted eastern sky, I remember to look for my old friends in the west, where the comparative darkness lets them put out a faint sparkle. Instead of focusing on the jets in a landing pattern to O'Hare that monotonously blaze a trail through the airspace over our subdivision, I glory in the gaudy Technicolor sunsets whose colors are enhanced by the dust in the atmosphere. The grit and grime particles in the air make the most beautiful lavender and pink celestial light shows before darkness drops her velvet curtain.

My backyard slopes slightly in the back, making an enclave of green that gives a sense of privacy. It's framed on one side by the neighbor's thirty-year-old weeping willow, which trails long leafy wands over our fence. If I don't look too closely, past it to their rusty shed, basketball hoop, and play set, I can almost imagine I am in the woods by a willow-walled stream somewhere.

69

When the windows are open at night, I can hear the gentle murmur of our neighbors' voices out on their patio, mingled with the distant barking of dogs and the rasping song of a cricket chorus tuning up. I miss the smell of honeysuckle blooming in the wildlife refuge across from which we lived in Tennessee that drenched the breezes with sweetness, and the spicy smell of horses that greeted me from the farm across the field. Now I inhale the pungent "green" aroma of a hundred mowed lawns, the soft fragrance of a multitude of flower beds filled with marigolds and petunias, and the tantalizing tang from barbecued chicken our neighbor Jim is grilling across the fence. The mixed essences trail in through the breeze that blows through my open window.

I expected the pace of the city to be more frantic. Instead, I have found myself juggling a surprising peace. Maybe it's the convenience of having a grocery store around the corner, the school a few blocks away, church a short trip by car. Music lessons and the orthodontist's appointment don't require scheduling a big chunk of the day just to travel there and back. The parks that surround us offer moments of quiet contemplation and opportunities for short walks between taxiing two teenagers to numerous activities.

From our front yard, I see skyscrapers in the distance. I drop my eyes and choose to look up close, soaking up the oaks and hickories that line the street with a cool presence like the satin inside a wool coat. As I walk my collie in the twilight, I breathe in trees, I absorb trees, I immerse myself in trees, I baptize myself in trees. Shadows of junk cars and plastic geese

70

in the yards fade out of view. The whitewashed Madonna in her grotto dissolves as I focus on the silken leaves of lambs' ears planted along the walk. The arrival of United Airlines flight #227 overhead is drowned by the "Cheer! Cheer! Cheer!" of the scarlet cardinal that flies just in front of me, announcing my arrival to—where? To whom? We circle the block as twilight creeps in. The color of the sky softens from silvery blue to pink stained with gray.

Back in the yard, in the dusk of the evening, I pull another herb plant out of the plastic flat and rough up its roots. Coercing it into the hole I've carved out of the unforgiving Illinois clay, I pour cold water and crush dirt around the base. It's up to its neck in earth. Ruthlessly, I pull off the withered bottom leaves. Suddenly, a late-day shaft of sun lights up the silvery thyme, illuminating it. Each leaf is suddenly glowing and incandescent. Its radiance defies its difficult place. Defiant. Yet compliant. Soon, its roots will penetrate the compacted clay, branching out, drawing energy and sustenance from its new home.

God, do you know what you are doing?

I pray for understanding, for patience. I pray for acceptance.

ARACHNOPHOBIA

Without Vigilance,
Unseen Things Creep In and Take Over

The doors of perception are hung with the
cobwebs of thought: prejudice, cowardice,
sloth.

EVELYN UNDERHILL

Ouch!

Something pricks me in my sleep, and I'm startled from the light unconsciousness of my dreams. My wrist is throbbing. Through half-opened eyes, I see a shadow scuttle across my hot wrinkled pillow and then disappear down the headboard in the dimness of the bedroom.

Spider bite.

Groggy, I rub the painful spot on my wrist. I wonder if the spider was traveling alone or as part of a tour group. As my eyes adjust to the darkness, I gingerly lift the covers, checking for any relatives or eight-legged friends that might be trailing behind. Nope. None—that I can see anyway. I turn the pillow over, looking for other invaders lurking in the moonlight. I run my hands over the top of the comforter, hoping I'll knock any other intruders onto the floor.

Nothing.

Sliding out from under the covers, I strip off my flannel pajamas, shake out each sleeve, then pull the pockets of the pants inside out. Picking up my pillow, I whap it against the wall a few times. I slip my pajamas back on, then I bend over and comb through my hair with my fingers—just in case.

I look over at Jeff, sound asleep and oblivious to the bedroom drama being enacted. I'm half tempted to wake him up

73

and enlist him in the hunt, but I charitably discard the thought. This time anyway.

Adjusting the pillow, I climb back into bed, rigid, wide-awake, wondering if anything else is lurking under the blankets. Sleep doesn't come easy.

In the morning, the bite on my wrist is a tiny welt, red and itchy, a reminder of the night's events. There are more than three thousand spider species in North America, but it's a safe bet that I was bitten by the common American house spider. It creeps out under the cover of darkness to spin its webs in nooks and crannies of houses, hoping to trap its victims in the sticky strands. Unlucky insects are swaddled in spider silk and carted off to another site, where the house spider injects them with venom and later eats them for breakfast.

The image—or rather the pain—of the house spider injecting me with venom is fresh in my mind. I try to imagine the quarter-inch arachnid mummifying me while I sleep, then hauling my middle-aged body into its net for its next meal— the stuff of B-grade movie nightmares—Jeff waking up in the morning, going to the bathroom to brush his teeth, and finding me trussed and hanging overhead, the main course for a spider brunch.

With a bit of investigation in the light of day, I notice the irregular cobwebs hung like hammocks in the corners of the ceiling and the crevices under my bed. From the look of the webs, and the amount of insects trapped in the tacky threads, they've been there for a long, long time. Festooned with dust as well as bugs, they are a definite discredit to my housekeeping skills. No wonder I've got spiders in my bed! Time to get busy.

I mount a posse, deputizing two reluctant teenagers and arming them with brooms and dusters. We spread out, walking through the house, knocking down gossamer mesh and cleaning out corners and baseboards. It's amazing how many webs there are. I realize how little I look at the ceiling, staircase treads, and the neglected corridor behind the piano. Even the light fixture in the dining room is draped with a few silken skeins.

Because of my lack of vigilance, undesirables have established themselves. A few threads here, a web or two there. Before I know it, I'm enmeshed in designs not of my own choosing. I wasn't paying attention to what was infiltrating my life, taking over my home.

But Lord, I hate housework. I'd rather dig in my garden than dust my bookcases, chat with a friend instead of vacuuming my carpets. Carpe diem. I seize the day and put blinders on to the chaos that ensues. I don't like the drudgery of dealing with tasks that are repetitious, yet I know in the back of my mind that it's important to do them if everything is going to run smoothly.

A pile of laundry is stacked four feet tall in the hall. "Let's go on a bike ride," I say to the kids. Dishes tower in the sink. I head out for a hike. I sit in the recliner reading a new library novel by the light filtering through sticky handprints on the windows. Dust bunnies of dog hair roll like tumbleweeds across the floor where I lie with my notebook, planning my garden for next spring.

At some point, even I know it's time to deal with the things I've let go—usually, when there is no clean underwear. Or the paper plates have come out too many times because all the dishes are in the sink. Maybe company is coming over, prompting a whirlwind housecleaning. Most of the time, I'm not motivated until there are painful consequences because of my inattention.

And the consequences of neglect can be harsh. My friend Scott was also bitten by a spider and didn't think anything of it. Slowly, over the weeks, the bite mark grew more angry looking, ringed by atrophied flesh. His worried wife insisted on taking him to the emergency room, where the doctors told him he had been bitten by a violin spider, more commonly known as the brown recluse spider. Like the house spider, the brown recluse enjoys living indoors, weaving loose, clingy webs in out-of-the-way places.

My Audubon field guide offers a caveat about the brown recluse: "This spider sometimes takes shelter in clothing or a folded towel and bites when disturbed. The wound commonly develops a crust and a surrounding red zone. The crust falls off, leaving a deep crater, which often does not heal for several months."

Hmm. I think of my friend. I examine my red spot again. No "crust" developing, I reassure myself. No "red zone." I chant "house spider, house spider, house spider" several times, reassuring myself with a protective mantra.

Hidden things. They come out and bite you when you least expect them to. They can fester and destroy. A little vigilance is maybe not a bad thing.

Normally spiders don't bother me; rather, they intrigue me—especially the big ones.

One summer while in New Orleans, I decide to ditch the wildlife in the French Quarter and explore the wildlife at the Barataria Preserve of Jean Lafitte National Historical Park and Preserve, a half hour drive away.

I stop by the ranger station to pick up a map, then head out on foot to hike along the boardwalks and dirt paths that ramble through a levee, a bayou, a swamp, a marsh, and a canal. In my Yankee ignorance, I'm not sure where one begins and another one ends. It's early morning, and I'm all alone.

Humidity wraps itself around me like a warm, wet dishcloth. Mosquitoes swarm in clouds, repelled by bug spray, looking for some square inch of my body that's not covered in chemicals.

As I step onto the boardwalk, I sense the presence of living things unseen. Out of the corner of my eye, I see something green slide up a tree. Spanish moss suddenly swings through the empty air, although there is no breeze. A branch cracks, and there's a glimpse of something furry that quickly disappears. There's a rustle in the palmettos. A single plant sways alone.

In the water, a carpet of duckweed ripples, something slithering and invisible swimming just beneath the surface. Small peat islands of plants I can't identify float by in the canal. The current is odd—moving one direction, then another, in a way that makes no sense. Tupelo and bald cypress trees emerge from the swamp, reaching for the light. Birds call, but most of their songs are strange to me.

77

Eyes examine me behind my back. I turn. No one's there. Clutching my pack, I move tentatively down the board-walk. Immediately I am enveloped by gummy fingers that caress my arms, trail across my cheeks, tangle my hair. Spun ropes cling to me like cotton candy in the humidity.

A golden-silk spider has spun a trellis across the path, and I'm the first one out this morning to hike and break the shimmering barrier. The web tendrils are as strong as fishing line, and it's impossible to get them off. I later find out that they really are that tough. Native Americans rolled together threads of golden-silk spider webs until they had the desired tensile strength for fishing lines and nets. No wimpy webs here.

I follow the trailing pieces of the shattered web I've ruined back to their origin: the wax myrtle next to the path. A golden-silk spider as big as my hand hangs by a thread in the midst of the destruction, her eight eyes glaring at me in primordial fury. The wreck of her web will cost her the rest of the day in repairs.

Sorry about that.

Squinting against the sun that drifts through the palmettos and cypress lining the boardwalk ahead, I see more diaphanous blockades: spectacular webs, three feet wide, slightly inclined orbs slung tightly across the path. The sunshine glints in the dew suspended on the notched support threads of their intricate mosaics. The sticky screens snag flying insects for future spider snacks.

Golden-silk spider silhouettes are everywhere, tattooed against the green-fringed blue sky. They loom overhead like trapeze artists, calicoed in reddish-orange, black, and white. Their heads are primitive tribal masks. Hanging upside down from the hubs of their webs, they watch my approach, worried about the destruction I might wreak on *their* homes. Vigilant.

And so am I as I move cautiously down the boardwalk, watching for more tricky traps. The air smells wet and pungently piney as I crush a sea grape underfoot. The humidity thickens the air, creating a moist soggy mist that's exhausting to breathe. Salty sweat beads down my spine and trickles in streams down the backs of my legs.

Cardinal lobelia grows along the trail, gashing the green foliage with its bloody scarlet spikes. A Carolina chickadee buzzes like a band saw from a nearby bald cypress. A cackling, booming sound echoes through the swamp. I check my steps, slowing down, uneasy. The haunting sound repeats, crescendos. Pig frogs, I find out later from the park ranger, but right now I don't know what is making the noise. Goosebumps prick my arms despite the heat. According to the ranger, pig frogs are as big as saucers, yet they are difficult to spot in the moist terrain.

The swamp is a lonely place, although full of life. It speaks of secrets, of hidden things. I'm not big on secrets, although I don't mind a little mystery from time to time. But I am uneasy with too much "not knowing," when there is more that is invisible than visible, when things crawl under your covers at night and bite. I want to bring them out into the bright light of day. Examine them. Identify them. I want to know what makes the noises, what spins the webs.

79

There's a great deal of mystery in living—a lot of things unseen. Some of those invisible things I'll figure out; other things will remain unknown. I'll have to accept that.

Meanwhile, I'm going to be vigilant about the unseen things that try to take up residence with me—choosy about what I allow, careful to eradicate what I don't want. I need to discriminate, perceive what I'm letting become a part of my life, making sure it's something I desire.

Hard work. Unenjoyable. But worth it.

FISHING AND THE ART OF SOUL MAINTENANCE

It's Important to Make Time to Do Nothing

The further the soul is from the noise of the world, the closer it may be to its Creator, for God, with His Holy angels, will draw close to a person who seeks solitude and silence.

THOMAS À KEMPIS

81

Sometimes I like to fish without bait. It gives the worms a day off and offers other folks the illusion that I am occupied with something industrious and worthwhile. There is implied permission, somehow, to sit quietly and do nothing without being questioned about it. It's more acceptable to say, "I'm going fishing" rather than, "I'm going to go sit for a while," or even the more lofty, "I am taking a spiritual retreat for personal reflection and meditation." Fishing is universally understood.

Lolling against a tree trunk with my line in the water, I can close my eyes and ponder a difficult situation. Untangling my line while untangling my problems. After a while, the snags in my soul begin to unsnarl a bit, loosen up, relax their tension. The little personal messes I've created begin to unknot.

My red and white bobber gently rides the ripples in the shady cove I'm tucked into on this lake, yet without any bait, perch and sunfish swim by uninterested. "We're not suckers," they mouth to me in fish bubbles on the surface. "You're going to have to give us something better than a bare size six gold Aberdeen hook, something with a little meat on it."

Fishing has not always been a contemplative activity for me. When I was in college, I had to take six physical education classes to graduate. Determined to make these a delightful antidote to some of the dry-as-dust courses mandated, I chose offbeat things I would enjoy. Fencing. Tap dancing. Pocket billiards. And—oh yeah—casting and angling.

This was fishing for the serious-minded, fishing for the informed. We studied the best ways to cast, the appropriate lures and bait, the right wrist movements, the proper fishing stance, fish identification, habitats. In the late fall hours, I spent class time casting my empty hook toward the red circle target on the field house floor. For one who had fished with her family from the cradle, this was a piece of cake.

For our final grade, we had to take a fishing trip and write a paper about our experience. It was November. It was cold. Nope, it was freezing.

My maternal grandparents are avid fishermen. Hearing of my plight, they offered to take me to one of our old fishing haunts. Setting out one frosty weekend morning, we loaded up their car with food and tackle boxes and headed for fish heaven. At the lake, we backed up Grandpa's handmade mahogany boat into the frigid water and unhitched it. A few sputters of the ignition, and we were off. After scouting promising locations, we found a secluded cove where we dropped our lines and settled down to wait.

The three of us, trying to stay warm, swigged hot tea from a thermos Grandma passed around. I was fishing with night-crawlers thick as my pinkie finger, hoping for something good to write about—hoping we would have some big hits quickly, so we could pack up and go home.

The sun disappeared in the metallic sky. An hour passed. Two hours. No bites. Toward noon, Grandma passed out homemade tuna-fish-on-wheat sandwiches and baggies full of potato chips, which we ate with blue lips and numb fingers. Three poles were in the water—and not a ripple to be found. The nightcrawlers lay curled in their perforated cottage cheese container, apathetic, like chilled dark spaghetti.

The afternoon wore on. Soft dampness patted my arms. Then, more insistently, wet flakes splatted against my cheeks. Snow was falling, coating the boat, our fishing tackle, and our bundled bodies with a thin crust of white.

Still no fish.

Grandpa and Grandma, firm believers in good grades and the value of a higher education, were made of stern stuff. If we had to shovel the snow out of the boat, we'd hang on until we caught a fish. They would aid their granddaughter in her quest for a college degree, even if it meant staying on the lake until it iced over and we had to chop holes in it in which to drop our hooks.

Soon, we exhausted the steaming liquid in the thermos. Despite the heavy clothes, sweaters, and blankets, I couldn't get warm. We cruised around the lake, looking for more promising spots, snow blowing around us, and came up empty.

Twilight. Then, the miracle. One pole bent almost double to the water, almost slipping out of my numb fingers.

I managed to write an "A" paper about catching one small crappie on my fishing trip. The professor gave me more credit for atmosphere than results.

For a long time in my life, fishing was a battle of wits. The end goal was measurable results. I've fished in Mexico, off the coast of Bermuda, and in the many lakes and ponds around my homes in Indiana, Tennessee, and now, Chicago. I've surf-fished in Florida and dropped hooks off docks in Michigan and Wisconsin lakes.

As I grow older, however, I find myself less enamored with the size and weight of my catch and more involved with the "atmosphere" of fishing—the time alone, the noticeable slowing down of my pulse as I disengage from the worries of meeting a deadline, tension with my teen-agers, or the pressure of completing some task that seems incredibly important.

With the first cast, the stress begins draining out of my neck, my back, my arms, my fingertips. As the day ambles on, my whole body relaxes. My mind unbends. By the time the sun begins its downward ramble toward the horizon, I find myself restored.

With this restoration comes appalling realization. I am horrified at how different I feel from when I started the day. Was I really wound that tight? Was I that tense? That wired? How do we get in the states we are in? The change takes place so gradually, so insidiously, that we don't even notice it until the day we slow down, take time off, and remember what peace feels like, what silence sounds like. What was the big rush?

85

John Ortberg must also feel this, for he notes, "Again and again as we pursue spiritual life, we must do battle with hurry. For many of us the great danger is not that we will renounce our faith. It is that we will become so distracted and rushed and preoccupied that we will settle for a mediocre version of it. We will just skim our lives instead of actually living them."

I'm going to slow down, I promise myself—and for a while I do. Armed with my fishing pole and bait-less hook, I pass a few hours in the company of random wildlife and my own vivid imagination, looking busy with the important work of fishing to those passing by. The best of both worlds—social acceptance and spiritual solitude. Pole in hand, I can lie on my back and watch cloud pictures form and dissemble like a slow-motion Etch-A-Sketch, while taking apart and putting together things that have eluded me in my hurried state of everyday affairs.

I can puzzle over the dragonfly poised at the edge of the reed canary grass. Is it a twelve-spot skimmer? Or a white tail? Study the patterns of light and shadow as the sun filters through the leaves of an oak. Enjoy the reflected light on the water, which acts as a shimmering disco ball, glinting lights across the banks. Watch a painted turtle cruise in the shallows by the shore.

Burly men with loaded bait buckets and state-of-the-art tackle boxes walk the deer path that crosses close to my fishing spot.

"Any bites?" they banter.

I shake my head ruefully. "Nope, not a nibble all day," I say. Inwardly, I smile.

86

They pause for a moment, shifting their poles from hand to hand, shaking their heads in sympathy, offering advice. I listen seriously, nodding sagely. I don't tell them that my Tupperware bait box is empty today. Wishing them luck, I avoid casting with my empty hook until they are well past my fishing hole.

Deceiving the world, my own little joke with God.

No worms will suffer agony today. Crickets and meal worms, minnows and nightcrawlers, rejoice! A breathing space for bass, a sabbatical for the sunnies, a fish furlough. Rings on the water tell me of missed opportunities under the very nose of my bobber. But I am satisfied, content to be complacent, happy in the fruitlessness of my fishing expedition.

At some point, I will gain the confidence to just rest and feed my soul. Until then, I lie back on the bank. Fishing for ideas, casting for inspiration, trolling for imagination. Trying to go deeper, finding out what lies just beneath the surface of my life.

Pole in the water, tree at my back, hook empty, I am content.

WINDS OF CHANGE

Loving What You Have,
Accepting What You Don't

If you can't hear the voice of the wind, you better learn.

THOMAS BERRY

The sound of the blinds banging by the bed jars me out of an uneasy sleep. Listening intently, I relax. No burglars, no child crying "Mommy" in the night. Only the wind. Jeff breathes softly next to me, oblivious to the night music crashing through the trees outside.

It's past midnight and now his birthday. Thirty-eight. Both of us battled proverbial midlife crises of one kind or another this past year, and we were appalled. A midlife crisis was one thing—we had assured ourselves—that would never touch us. We joked about it, poked fun at the red sports cars his coworkers purchased, agonized over the dissolution of a friend's marriage, murmured sympathetically over our neighbor's brushes with career shake-ups. But when the winds of midlife crashed through our own lives, we were bowled over.

A search for identity. A search for meaning. Why is midlife such a time of upheaval?

Midlife and marriage. It's amazing when you love someone so much but wake up in surprise next to a stranger in your bed. Who is that guy you went home with sixteen years ago? Whose children you delivered? Whose clothes you've washed, dinners you've cooked, dreams and disappointments you've shared?

Suddenly, I'm speaking Chinese and he's speaking Norwegian. We read things into the nuances of a raised eyebrow, a certain look. I fly off the handle at every little thing. He wonders where the familiar person he loved has disappeared to. We both feel helpless to change.

I read books. I wonder if my faith is enough. I talk to friends. I sort myself out. I pray a lot but wonder if anyone is listening.

There is something about midlife that beckons us to dig deeper, to find our true identity, to explore who we really are. To ask questions, where before we just accepted. To doubt, where before we blindly believed. To look back over our lives and yearn for a new direction, a different path.

Sue Monk Kidd must have felt some of this as well: "When change-winds swirl through our lives, especially at midlife, they often call us to undertake a new passage of the spiritual journey: that of confronting the lost and counterfeit places within us and releasing our deeper, innermost self—our true self. They call us to come home to ourselves, to become who we really are."

My true self. Just what is my true self anyway? Thoughts whirl together like forbidden fruits in a blender.

I want to flirt with strangers in a sidewalk café in Paris, wade into a cold trout stream in Montana, stroll along warm, dusty streets in a border town in Mexico, float down the Amazon River, threatened by crocodiles, terrorized by terrorists.

I want to climb a mountain that's never been climbed. I want to taste danger like hot acid rising in my throat. I want to sleep in the desert with the stars scattered like glitter over my head, traipse through the outback, chase chance down a narrow street in Greece, where the sun bleaches the white buildings by the Aegean Sea, scorching them with heat.

Instead, I plan what we'll have for dinner—chicken or spaghetti, or shall we order pizza again? I map out car pools, I dutifully finish my assignments, I dry dishes, I fold laundry, I vacuum carpets that monotonously collect dust and dog hair an hour later to be vacuumed again.

I want to raft rapids and instead float on a still pond. I want to taste pomegranates, and taste only tapioca.

I want. I want. I want.

Oh, these bright faces that look at me, trustingly, longingly, secure in my love for them and my stability. Could any of these other things be better than this?

No. Only in my imagination. But sometimes I wonder.

So many of the things I always thought I would do won't materialize. Reality means embracing the things I've been given. Grieving the losses. Celebrating the things I love, the good things I never expected, the things I take for granted. Admitting that my life might be different than I planned and making my peace with it.

I feel hot—a hot flash?—Oh, Lord!—and restlessly turn over my pillow, plumping it for coolness. A rush of air curls around the house in an extended exhalation, making the bedroom window curtains lift and fall.

The wind is blowing violently tonight, and it makes me tense. Most of my life has been spent as a Midwesterner, naturally wary of the wind. Distrustful of it. Alert. On guard. Anyone who has lived with the wind's capriciousness knows it can change in a moment. It's not reliable.

One of my earliest memories is the wail of the tornado siren and my mother frantically calling me to come to the closet in the basement as the wind sucked like a vacuum around our home. Trembling, I clung to my yarn rag doll and waited with my brother and sister for the all clear, while Mom stood at the upstairs window, scanning the skies.

I still feel that terror from time to time. In *Wind*, Jan DeBlieu writes that psychologists say windstorms may indeed leave lasting scars.

> Residents of cohesive, family-oriented communities seem to fare better psychologically after windstorms than people living far from their families or alone in big cities. Those who are mentally unstable by nature have the most difficult time putting their lives back together. But in a study of victims of a 1989 tornado in Huntsville, Alabama, therapists found that many well-adjusted people also suffered prolonged mental distress. For years afterward they would become extremely nervous in high wind.

The wind, the wind. We can't see it, just its effects. It comes from nowhere and blasts us off our foundations. We are buffeted, blown around, bashed about. It leaves lasting scars. Sometimes, it destroys everything we have.

Watching early screenings of *The Wizard of Oz*, seeing Dorothy whisked away from everything she loved, added to my childhood fear of the wind. Even as an adult, I often wake, sweat-drenched, after a nightmare in which a tornado separates me from Jeff and my two kids. These nightmares are not without a grounding in reality.

I stood one sultry July Sunday in a long checkout line in a large Indiana discount store, uncomfortable in my church clothes, ready to pay for a few last-minute items. Clouds were piling up on the horizon, and I was impatient to beat the storm and get a little gardening in before the threatened deluge. Jeff and our two young children were trying on footgear at Payless, a few stores down in the shopping strip, the outcome of complaints about pinched toes in dress shoes that morning. I checked my watch impatiently as the line slowly snaked forward.

The store loudspeaker blared, and a woman's voice clipped out words over the intercom. "All associates: code black!"

I looked at the teenage cashier, whose face had turned the color of skim milk. "Code black?" I said curiously. "What's that?"

"Tornado," she said. "We've got to move to the center of the store."

My family. It was all I could think about. I threw my purchases on the floor and raced for the electronic doors at the front of the store as cashiers and customers fled to the center aisles for cover.

Could they have gone to the van? I raced through the parking lot. The wind tore at me, howling, its hot breath mixed with sharp pieces of icy hail that pricked my skin. A greenish light cast eerie reflections on the car windows around me. A siren wailed in the distance. I reached our van.

Empty.

I yelled their names, but the wind tore the words from me and sent the sound skittering away. In the distance, I heard an unearthly thundering, the proverbial freight train coming. Fear gripped me in a vise.

Where could they be?

A shout from the sidewalk. The kids, alarmed, calling my name.

"Mommy! Mommy!"

With relief, I ran to where they stood with Jeff and gathered them in my arms, tears mingling with the first angry raindrops pelting the plaza. Desperately seeking shelter, we slipped into a clothing store, where customers and clerks huddled in the flimsy bathroom. Looking over my head, I was struck by the shoddy construction. Some protection.

The wind screamed. The tornado was coming closer. Jenny's eyes were big in the flickering electricity, like a deer's eyes caught in the shine of a car's headlights. A skinny middle-aged woman jammed next to me began to moan, then to cry. Her elementary-aged children were at home, left for a few moments while she ran an errand.

I found myself praying out loud, my voice sounding hollow in the small room. No one objected. We huddled, terrified, praying. If there were any atheists in the room, they were pondering a quick conversion.

The building shook. The winds howled. The storm wailed past.

The radio, tuned to a local station, announced an all clear. Cautiously, we crept out of the bathroom, wove around the clothes racks, and walked out to the parking lot, to a van peppered with melting hail. We drove desperately for home, hoping our house would still be there.

We were fortunate. Our house had survived the storm. Limbs had been torn from our silver maples in the front yard, and there was some minor mutilation to our dogwood tree in the back. Other families had not fared as well. The tornado had blown apart a barn in the field behind our home, skipped over our house, then ravaged houses and trailers in the country fields across the road, blowing them apart, turning them into confetti. Insulation was draped from poplar trees like pink and yellow Spanish moss. Roof shingles were plastered against wire fences.

Miraculously, no one had been killed. Many, however, were homeless, left without their necessities, their photographs, their pets, and their memories.

Now, as the wind blows around the house, I lie in the dark, thinking about my family. I remember the terror of almost losing those I love so much. I think about the winds that are blowing through my life.

The winds have hit me already, but I sense there will be more temptations, more storms. I will be buffeted by things yet to come. Somehow, I need to stay anchored. To remember what I have. To avoid being obsessed with my "wants." To discard my selfishness without losing my sense of adventure, my desire to grow and learn. To accept what I've been given with gratitude.

To come through the storms unscathed. To live unafraid of the wind.

PRAIRIE FIRE

How Suffering Can Bring About Growth

Like the snow on the stark spruce limb coated with ice, then stripped by wind, we melt away and return again. Stronger for the tempering flame.

BRUCE COCKBURN

96

It's the last day of February, and parking lot 25 is full of cars. Darn it! I treasure my daily walk on the Schulenberg Prairie at the Morton Arboretum—especially the solitude during the winter months. Must be a class field trip. I contemplate walking the east woods instead, but the pull of the prairie is irresistible. Sighing, I pull my battered car into the gravel lot.

As I stride down the asphalt maintenance road that leads to the prairie, my nose begins to twitch. The light breeze brings the smell of smoke to my nostrils. The old field along the path, once a flat tablecloth of dried Queen Anne's lace and parched goldenrod's intricate seed heads, is smoldering. Black scorched earth and ashes form a desolate platform for charred branches poking up from the ground. Song sparrows dart past me, chirping anxiously.

Quickening my steps, I hike to where the asphalt ends and an old two-track leads to the prairie. The savanna, a mixing zone of grasses and trees, breathes gray fumes. A honey locust tree exhales puffs of smoke from its blackened bark. Ahead, I hear crackling. As I round the curve, I see the flames.

The Schulenberg Prairie is on fire. What yesterday was one hundred acres of buttery bleached Indian grass and airy, ribboned switchgrass today is fuel for an inferno that licks over its surface in an ever moving wall of flame.

Every year, sections of the Schulenberg Prairie are burned by the staff at the arboretum. Although to the casual observer it looks as if the prairie is being destroyed, the prairie's trial by fire transforms and rejuvenates it. Hot flames stimulate some of the wildflower seeds to germinate and bloom. As vegetation burns, the ground is coated with powdery black ash, which heats the ground in the late winter sunshine and brings forth new growth in early spring. Fire destroys invasive weeds and invites the prairie grasses to spread out and flourish.

Tallgrass prairie once spanned much of the Central Plains. Fired by lightning, and later, Native American hunters, a prairie burned quickly. Within weeks it was an emerald fuzz of green shoots that attracted buffalo and wildlife. Due to the fires Native Americans set, the eastern forest was kept at bay.

In the past millennium, most of the tallgrass prairie that covered the middle United States fell to agriculture and the plow. What once was a rich diversity of sun-drenched compass plants, purple coneflowers, and big bluestem is now tilled, chemically dependent monocultures of corn and wheat. In recent years, realizing that prairies were slipping away to extinction, volunteers and conservancy groups have worked to restore and preserve what is left. The Schulenberg Prairie is one such treasure.

Using my binoculars to penetrate the smoky haze, I see a troop of twenty-five men and women in yellow slickers, murmuring into walkie-talkies and igniting patches of grass with their drip torches. A water truck hovers in the background, ready to rush in should the fire turn recalcitrant. Although the burning seems random to me at first glance, a pattern emerges. The burn is set so the flames run to the firebreak—in this case, the gravel two-track—where they smolder and quickly extinguish. Once a portion of acreage is blackened, the team walks into the wind, then begins to set a line of fire again. The flames sweep down the slope toward the burned area, which now serves as a natural barrier.

A mown path boxes the outlines of the acreage, keeping the fire a manageable distance from the surrounding subdivision. Yet stories are told of previous fires that leapt the mown path and crossed into backyards. Sometimes, the fires burn seemingly out of control.

The wind is tricky today and variable. With both uneasiness and fascination I watch the blaze move closer to where I stand, riveted. I try to tear my gaze away from the blaze, but like a motorist rubbernecking at a traffic accident, I am helpless to look anywhere else.

Liquid flame whips up twenty feet, thirty feet, forty feet into the sky, where it dissolves in an oily vapor that makes the air shimmer and waver. Ashes dance through the smoke. The wind presses the heat from the flames into my body like a hot iron. The fire nears.

Popping, snapping, and crackling sounds, like a hundred frantic cats in a paper grocery bag, punctuate the air around me. The wind brings an undercurrent of rustling and hissing to my ears as it blows through the dried-out big bluestem and Indian grass clumps yet untouched.

I watch my memories of the past year fuel the flames. Up goes the clump of prairie cordgrass I always watch for when I walk the trampled path that meanders through the bur oaks. The flattened stands of New England asters and stiff golden-rod that mark the deer beds are gone now; only slight depressions in the ground remain to show the deer's nighttime hide-aways. The bridge over Willoway Creek, where I often rest and toss the chipmunks my apple cores, takes on a ghostly aspect through the curling smoke that shrouds it in greenish browns. The coneflower seed heads, which give off a lemony fragrance when I crush them between my fingers, are reduced to soft white ashes sprinkled on soot. Purple prairie clover's cylinderic seed heads are prime fodder for the blaze, as are the bunches of feathered little bluestem in the sandy soil.

Other memories burn away in my mind. A friend who died at Christmas, cancer consuming her body and most of her spirit, leaving her two children motherless. The father of our daughter's preschool playmate who went into his garage, put his shotgun in his mouth, and pulled the trigger. Our neighbors who waved to us the morning they drove off for their vacation, smiling and happy. They never saw the drunk in the pickup truck who crossed the median.

Up in smoke. Suffering purifies us, the questions that pour forth define us. Our unknowing makes us pace the floor at night, alternately shaking our fist at God and begging him to hold us close, to tell us everything will be all right, that someday it will all make sense. We scream as the flames lick us, begging for mercy. Are you there, God? Why is this happening?

100

Ashes, ashes, we all fall down.

I wonder if the two courting song sparrows I listened to yesterday escaped the burn. The male's melodic trebles and trills had caused me to stretch out on the bridge and lay my head on my pack. I was lulled by the chanting—an uncomplicated prairie lullaby that swept the cobwebs of work pressures of the day out of my head. What of the voles and shrews, known to me only by their tiny footprint trails that peppered the snowy paths I walked in January? Were they charred skeletons? Or had they survived to breed and populate the prairie again?

The coyote, which I knew only by his tracks and his chalky gray scat, doubtless had outrun the conflagration. Muskrats whose prints embossed the powdered snow on the frozen creek in December are safely tucked in their hollows under the tree roots perforating the bank.

I close my eyes, erasing the flames all around me. Summer will come again and with it a new creation. I will run through acres of grass alongside the creek that cuts a watery blue-green scribble through the flowering fields. The eastern meadowlark will bring forth silvery notes of gladness in praise of the day. Slivers of yellow petals from the flowering grasses will dust my purple fleece jacket. The smell of mountain mint will wash the clean, fresh air. The roughness of prairie dock leaves will sandpaper my legs. Switchgrass sprays will catch the light, their seeds sparkling like water droplets suspended against a porcelain sky. Big bluestem's turkey-footed trinity of seed spikes will cleave the air, waving triumphantly in the wind.

Oh, ghost, you are not dead! You have arisen! It is the resurrection! Alleluia. Amen.

Yea, though I walk through the valley of the shadow . . . I will lie down in grass, I will rest my head on pillows of prairie dropseed, I will look up, up, up—eight feet, ten feet over my head—where splotches of blue sky are patched around the Indian grass plumes. I will listen to the rustle of white-footed deermice around me, cautiously scampering through the layer of dead leaves where I rest. The smell of grass . . . The feel of grass . . . I will immerse myself in it. I will drink in its colors. Lavender, pink, gold, blue—a sunset rainbow painted in grass.

Blackened bits of big bluestem waft through the air. It's difficult to breath. The fire creeps closer. I tuck my binoculars into my pack and turn to go. Tomorrow I will walk the desolate black landscape, looking for signs of new growth and rejuvenation rising from the holocaust. The earth, covered with dark cinders, will heat quickly and stimulate the beautiful prairie wildflowers to germinate. With the heavy mat of dead foliage and weeds removed, carpets of pink shooting stars will spangle the dark earth. Vanilla grass will spread sweet fragrance in the air. Stripped bare, seared, the prairie will bring forth new growth. Verdant. Fecund. Diverse. Alive.

Some of what is gone was beautiful, meaningful. Some of it was useless and invasive, preventing further growth. Something new is being created out of this hellish inferno. Something beautiful is on the way.

But for now, only desolation.

Walking back to the parking lot through the smoke, I start the car and drive home. The rest of the day I am quiet, thinking over the day's events.

Two A.M. I wake to the sound of a gentle rain falling. I close my eyes again but smile in the darkness. On the prairie, new life is stirring.

CABIN FEVER

In the Darkest Night,
There Is the Hope of Morning

Will my eyes adjust to this darkness? In the
dark, is it best to wait in silence?

NICHOLAS WOLTERSTORFF

Almost midnight. The porch swing creaks back and forth under the weight of my sleepy body, wrapped in a baby blue chenille blanket pulled from the bed a few moments ago. It's June, but the weather at this northern Michigan lake is wintry and wet. The wind began rising today and now howls around our rented vacation cabin. It squeezed through the cracked window frames, causing me to toss and turn in the uncomfortable bed.

Sleepless, cranky, I gingerly slipped out from between the sheets, pulling one of the covers around me in the refrigerated air. Our aging collie, sleeping at the foot of the bed, stirred and woke, then resignedly pulled herself to her feet to follow me.

After padding barefoot across the living room to the kitchen, careful not to wake my son who is sleeping on the pullout couch, I quietly set the kettle on the stove burner to brew some herbal tea—my time-proven defense against night terrors. When the kettle whistled tentatively, I turned off the stove and plopped my Celestial Seasonings tea bag into a cracked mug from the cabinet. Cradling the steaming mug in my hands, I draped the covers around me like a fluffy toga and groped through the darkness, out the aged door and across the boarded porch floor to the swing, where I could rock alone with my thoughts.

The wind whistles through the leaves of the ancient willow tree just beyond the porch with a sound like an exuberant boy blowing across the top of a pop bottle. It sneaks through the cheesecloth holes of the screened-in porch and blows the steam from my hot peppermint tea back in my face, first warming me, then giving me chills from the moisture that clings to my cheeks.

The night sky is dark wet slate; the clouds lie flat like crisp ironed sheets, with barely a wrinkle. Not a single star penetrates the smothering overcast. Whitecaps foam and froth on the lake spread out in front of me, churned and whipped by wind. The knotted rope that hangs from a sturdy branch in the willow by the cabin is a swinging shadow against the background of the lake. An aluminum rowboat, securely double-tied against the wind and waves, slams against the dock.

Our beach towels sag on the clothesline slung between two trees, barely moving in the gusting wind. Wet, sodden, they weigh down the line like cement. Swimsuits, dishcloths, T-shirts—in this weather, nothing on the line will be dry by morning.

The waves slurp at the shore. Raindrops splat and ping in the pots and pans we hastily put under the roof leaks on the porch, their tinging as monotonous as a metronome.

I wrap my arms around my knees and swing in the dark. I feel sad, and I don't know why.

> Ah, awful weight! Infinity
> Pressed down upon the finite Me!

My anguished spirit, like a bird,
Beating against my lips I heard;
Yet lay the weight so close about
There was no room for it without.
And so beneath the weight lay I
And suffered death, but could not die.

An angry gust of wind buffets the cabin, and something crashes inside. The dog gets up from her vigil alongside the glider and barks a warning. I hear one of the kids stir for a moment, mumble. Silence. They are too tired from their day on the lake to wake up completely.

It was not a good day. Our tempers were snarled like the fishing line and tackle lying on the windowsill. We were frazzled by the cold, drizzly weather that permeated our skimpy shorts and sleeveless shirts and frustrated by the too-close quarters, the sudden family togetherness after the structure of school and work. Jeff finally took the kids away from the cabin and left me alone for a while so we could sort ourselves out and start over. Family vacations—so much hoped for, such high expectations.

A little votive candle sits on the windowsill next to a book of matches, left over from the dinner decorations we used to try to make our meal more festive. I light the candle for companionship. It flickers in its glass holder as the wind drafts over it, trying to snuff it out. The edges of the holder are just high enough to keep it burning.

I swing back and forth. Night. It sends me prowling around the cabin, curling up on the couch, slipping outside. I stave

107

off dark thoughts with hot herbal tea, a companionable book, the armor of a well-worn afghan, the flickering light of a small candle. These are paltry weapons against the dark.

Thoughts come unbidden. Verses from a Brooks Williams song circle through my mind:

> The ghost of indecisiveness
> The skeleton of past regrets
> Meet in my hallway
> Dance on my steps
> Waiting at the foot of my bed
> Night Fears.

Night is a measureless merry-go-round of endless inquiry. I turn over and over things I've said, wrong things done, thoughts better left unearthed. My fears for myself, my family, the future. Mistakes I've made. What I hide in the light haunts me by night. The specters of the unconscious glide out from locked boxes and line up. One by one in the spotlight they stroll across the stage and mock my insufficiency. My shellacked self by day, my naked vulnerability in the dark.

> In the wee hours
> Before the dawn
> I remember too clearly
> Everything that's gone on
> Waiting at the foot of my bed
> Night Fears.

Early this morning, I looked up from the porch to see two young girls coming toward the cabin. They were both dirty and barefoot, with blonde hair that tangled like pond weed down their backs. The younger of the two carried something in her hands. Tentatively, they beckoned to me where I sat on the porch, and, full of curiosity, I went to see.

Cupped in the older one's hands was a baby bird, only a few inches long, its every vein etched in stark prominence in blue against its peach-colored skin. With each breath, a few pathetic unformed feathers trembled briefly.

The girls, eagle-eyed, had spotted the tiny baby on the road as they bicycled to the lake. The same wind that whipped me now had blown this morning and most likely knocked it from a tree. The bird was blind and helpless. They had instinctively picked it up and looked for the nest—nowhere to be found. Cradling the bird, they had walked their bikes to the nearest cabin, seeking advice.

They didn't know what to do, and neither did I. To my experienced adult eyes, the fledgling didn't have a chance. I opened my mouth to discourage them, but the words died on my lips in the face of the trusting hope on the two smudged faces in front of me. We settled on taking a basket from the cupboard and filling it with paper napkins, then setting it on the top of our coffeemaker, where—hopefully—the Lilliputian bird would stay warm. The girls, satisfied, decided to leave the bird with me until they finished their day's business of fishing and swimming at the lake. Later, they trundled it home, the wicker basket swinging from their bicycle handlebars, the baby bird still holding on to life by a thread. They were confident it would survive, fed on hand-dug worms and beetles pulled from under their woodpile, sleeping atop their own coffeemaker amid three family cats.

I remember being young and optimistic, sure that with the right care and nurturing, everything would turn out right. I feel old, jaded. I've seen too many disappointments, too many deaths.

I think about the baby perch we caught that afternoon off the pier. The kids brought it to me, concerned because it had swallowed the hook. No matter how far down I reached, I couldn't pull the hook out. We cut the hook and released it, gills bloody, back into the lake. We later found it floating, dead, and I berated myself for not putting it out of its misery. Yet I had strung the worm on the hook that attracted it in the first place. Had the worm been in pain as I pushed the silver metal through its segmented body?

Life is fragile. So much death and suffering goes on right under our noses. Things as simple as the fly that flew into the hot cooking oil I was heating on the stove while fixing dinner. It shuddered, died in—agony? Do flies feel? Would God the Creator give feelings to insects? To worms? To fish? To birds?

Sometimes we play a role in the suffering. Sometimes we feebly try to alleviate it. Sometimes we are only observers, helpless to make a difference. How much suffering happens that we don't know about? How much suffering have I caused that I don't know about? I've caused enough that I *do* know about . . .

110

Everything I've done, everything I've said
Everything I hope for, everything I dread
Real or imagined, future or past
Good thing I know that night don't last
Night Fears.

So many nights I feel I am just marking time. Waiting for morning. Can I trust that it will come?

It's hard to let go of my fears. It's hard to trust when it's dark. It's hard to hope.

I'm waiting for the sun to break through the darkness, trying to hold on.

I think of St. Teresa of Avila:

So let us not trouble ourselves about our fears,
nor lose heart at the sight of our frailty,
but humbly remind ourselves that without the grace of God
we are nothing.
And then, distrusting our own strength,
let us commit ourselves to His mercy.
Follow Jesus into the Garden of Gethsemane and on to
    Calvary.
And only then, to Easter morning.

In a few hours, the gold of sunrise will underline the dark clouds, chasing away the ghosts of my night thoughts, clearing up my confusion. The sun will split the darkness like an ax splitting wood, cleaving it cleanly in two.

111

I know the light is coming. I'm clinging to the thought. It seems so far away.

So I wait.

Waiting and waiting for morning, waiting and waiting for morning.

Swinging on the porch, alone in the dark, waiting.

13

How Does Your Garden Grow?

Building Faith through Community

Mary, Mary, quite contrary, how does your garden grow?

Nursery rhyme

I'm working in my prairie patch in my backyard, humming my favorite Neil Young song and growing more and more annoyed. For the past hour, I've been trying to figure out which green shoots are going to grow up to be big tallgrass prairie plants like bluestem and which ones are *Poa pratensis*, Kentucky bluegrass, and must be ruthlessly ripped out. Bluegrass and bluestem. The names are so close you'd think they were siblings, but the full-grown plants will be only distantly related.

The afternoon sun is hot, and I'm sweating enough to wring a bucketful of saltwater out of my T-shirt and shorts. Mud cakes my boots and turns my fingernails into crescents of black grit. I tossed the gardening gloves off minutes after I started my weed patrol. Good intentions, but I like the feel of the earth on my hands. I don't think Martha Stewart would approve.

Sighing, I lie flat on my stomach on the swampy ground, trying to get a worm's-eye view of a small clump of . . . something. Little bluestem? If I leave it, and I'm wrong, these slender blades could turn into a monster weed, taking over with vegetative vengeance. If I pull it—and it's little bluestem—I've lost a year's head start. I'm tentative. It's like looking at baby pictures of Marilyn Monroe and not having a clue as to what the mature specimen would look like.

Trying not to get muddy fingerprints all over the pages, I consult my prairie book, which shows six- and seven-foot mature stands of prairie grasses. Sheesh. Nothing in my small patch looks like it could achieve the potential shown in these photos.

A shadow falls across the grasses, and I look up, peering into the sun. A weather-beaten figure stands silhouetted against the sky. It's Gerry, my backyard neighbor to the west. Gerry wrote the definitive book on plants of the Chicago region a few years back and knows every stem, flower, and leaf blade in DuPage County. He worked for many years at the Morton Arboretum and helped plant the Schulenberg Prairie. His own yard is a wild assortment of native plants in prairie and savanna-like settings.

Like the western heroes of old, he's here to help. Hang on, little lady. Let the big guns ride to the rescue.

I explain my dilemma. Gerry immediately crouches down beside me, intent on figuring out the situation. His expertise makes short shrift of my indecision. With ruthless concentration, he begins pulling plants, calling out their Latin names as he tosses them into the nearby compost pile. This, he says, is an invasive nonnative—*Barbarea vulgaris*, yellow rocket. Zip! Into the compost pile. Off go the roots and shoots of crabgrass. We pull up sprawling starts of chickweed, *Stellaria media*. Out comes henbit, with its petite, orchid-like amethyst flowers. Infant maple tree sprouts that wandered over from a neighboring yard meet their demise.

115

Then he introduces me to my big bluestem, planted last summer. Look at the hairy base, he extols. See the wine-red color of the stem. Once he points it out, it does look different from the other grasses and weeds. It's been in front of my eyes the whole time, but I needed someone to clarify and explain. I tenderly press the soil a little firmer around the clumps.

We continue yanking. Working in companionable silence, things begin to come into focus. I can see the good, the bad, and the ugly.

Then Gerry pauses for a moment, for the first time indecisive. This, he says, is nimblewill, *Muhlenbergia schreberi*, a native grass that's drifted into my prairie, but not a typical resident of tallgrass prairie patches. It's up to me—do I want it?

I stop to think, then decide to discard it. I have to be choosy about what I let inhabit my small plot. Yank! Off to the compost pile.

It's difficult to decide what stays and what is ruthlessly eradicated. But a few words from a friend make my life so much easier in my garden—and in my faith. So often in both, I try to do everything myself. I want to be in control, to have all the answers. I want to be tough, resilient. I sleep in on Sunday morning, thinking I'll do devotions at home, a little prayer time later. I forget my need for companions on the journey, those who have a viewpoint different from my own, those who see faith through a more experienced lens. I need someone to bounce ideas off, someone with whom to share my questions and explore new territory.

Thomas à Kempis reminds me, "No one is wholly self-sufficient, no one has enough wisdom by himself. That being the case, we must support and comfort each other; help, teach and advise one another."

I like to think that my garden is my own creation, yet it is also a conglomeration of my friends' gardens. I'm reminded of this when I'm working outside one muggy Sunday afternoon and Mike, my hosta-and-bedding-plant friend, phones me with an enticement: "Hey, I'm cleaning up my garden beds. Want to come and get some stonecrop and vinca I'm throwing out?"

Breaking the speed limit, I zoom over in my car. I'm there in minutes, tenderly troweling up his outcasts and putting the orphans in a cardboard box. Returning home, I transplant them into a shady corner of my backyard. His excess becomes another stanza in the symphony of my garden.

Later that afternoon, I wander over to Gerry's in search of a plant identification that is eluding me. Gerry's wife, Margaret, and his twenty-something son, Dave, are leaning on shovels, deep in conversation, contemplating a battalion of burlap-bagged prairie plants slung all over the backyard. Gerry, they tell me, is off hobnobbing with prairie aficionados in Iowa, and they are left to place these plants before his return home.

I show Margaret my problem plant, which all my garden books seem to have forgotten, and she immediately identifies it as *Hesperis matronalis*, dame's rocket. Margaret has picked up a lot of plant ID's by osmosis, living with Gerry, and is a gentle encyclopedia of nature information.

The mystery solved, we turn our attention to the plants, which Dave says were rescued from sudden annihilation by bulldozing. Apparently, one of Gerry's restoration clients decided to put in $200,000 worth of bluegrass turf and get rid of his native plants, which he had tired of. And these salvaged specimens are no wee bairns. They are monster prairie plants, Arnold Schwarzenegger plants. Plants that could shade a small house. Rattlesnake master clumps as big as dinner plates. Shooting stars the size of galaxies.

We all shake our heads, bemused over the shortsightedness of the client. Some people have so much yet don't know what they have. I offer to help them put the rescued survivors in their new homes. We work a few hours, absorbed in the happy task of placing plants. When I leave, muddy and content a few hours later, I have been gifted with rattlesnake master starts and a large bouquet of spiderwort seedlings.

I reluctantly refuse the shooting stars Dave offers. My prairie patch is pretty shady. The shooting stars are so spectacular that the idea of putting them in a place they might sulk is too disconcerting. There are some things my immature garden is not equipped to handle yet, some things that would die in the climate of my backyard. Maybe in a few years I'll have the right spot for them. But right now, I'm not ready.

I'm going to regret it, I bet. But I feel greedy just taking what I do. Celestial plants! Heaven on earth. Pure bliss.

After we make a date for them to come over and dig out some of my arrowhead plants for their pond-in-progress, I trundle my newcomers down the slope to my backyard. Gently, I place them in their new, hastily selected spots and water them in. With the addition of the new arrivals, my prairie patch takes on a more mature look. From infancy to toddlerhood in a matter of hours.

The phone rings as I'm washing the dirt off my hands and the sun is dipping low behind the trees. It's Cathy, my neighbor down the street. She's thinning out her wild columbines—would I like some? I grab my trowel and a plastic bucket and head for her house. We chat while I excavate columbines, a spectrum of burnt oranges and apricots. While I dig, Cathy casually mentions how much she admires my variegated hostas, something that came gratis with our house when we bought it. I happily offer her a few in trade, and we pick up the columbines and trek down the street to shovel some plants out of my front yard.

My hostas were choking each other anyway, battling over their crowded strip of turf. Thinned out, they stretch their leaves, looking relieved. A piece of my garden is now resting in Cathy's, and her columbines will become a piece of my own botanical crazy quilt.

That night, as I'm sponging off in the tub, I ponder the day. The dirt swirling and blackening the water around me comes from four different gardens. The terra firma under my nails includes the black soil of Gerry's prairie, the trucked-in topsoil of Mike's backyard, the grainy grit of Cathy's rock garden, and my own clay real estate. My yard, so carefully planned and gridded on paper, has gone off on a carefree drunken binge, a torrid tangent in twenty-four hours.

Flexible, open to change. The landscape of my life fluctuates, bends, stretches. The original concept is there—framed in my limestone-edged beds—but the final result is not at all what I intended. People will admire my garden, not realizing what a hodgepodge patchwork of different input it has received.

My friends help me prop some things up here, give a little advice there, work with me to root out any ugliness that crops onto the scene. We sift through the questions together, and I make more confident decisions. I'm not always in the right place to handle what they can give. But because of them, new things I hadn't planned on will bloom and prosper in the ongoing mural that is my backyard.

A quantum leap in the garden today. The beneficiary of this suburban swap meet. As darkness falls, I look over my miniature landscape in process, satisfied, anticipating the next unexpected adventure. That's how I like it. That's how my garden grows.

14

AFTER DARK

Hatred Is Easy;
Forgiveness Is Not Impossible

Your search for true healing will be a suffering search. Many tears still need to be shed. But do not be afraid. The simple fact that you are more aware of your wounds shows that you have sufficient strength to face them.

HENRI J. M. NOUWEN

Sometimes nothing seems quite as satisfying as cold, clean hatred—especially when you have been treated unjustly. There's something imminently enjoyable about savoring the unfair words that were spoken, rolling the incident over in your mind, tasting the bitterness again and again. You suck on the memory like a sour lemon drop. You probe the old wound, as your tongue probes the empty socket of a tooth recently extracted by the dentist. You remind yourself of how grievous the world can be.

The sun is setting, and I'm sitting on the banks of a marsh, wrapped in my purple fleece jacket, muffled with a scarf against the winter cold, replaying in slow motion the conversation I had with someone I thought was a friend. I brood over the words that were said, that cut like the bone-chilling December wind slicing through me now. As I remember, hatred courses through me in a rush.

I shift on the icy hard ground, trying to get comfortable, camouflaged in the cattails and phragmites that line the muddy edges of the water's expanse. This spot is a good getaway—only a few minutes from my doorstep, in a forest preserve tucked into a pocket of businesses and a swath of highways. It's the perfect place to host a private pity party. I break off a blade of canary grass and twirl it in my fingers, then slowly tear it to bits.

A few mallards glide along the water by my secret refuge, pausing once in a while to pull some tender roots out of the icy mud. A pair of northern shovelers coasts by, flaunting their scoop-shaped bills and surprising me with a new addition to my bird list. The sun begins to drop behind the high-rise office building in the distance, the tangerines blending with the blues, bruising the sky in an ever dimming twilight. I hear a muffled sound of commuters on their way home from work, pulling in at the Wal-Mart parking lot across the highway.

I think over the troubling conversation again. How humiliated I felt. Yet I'm sure no one around me knew. I laughed to hide my distress. I'm an expert at covering up my true feelings.

Despite the cold, hot tears course down my cheeks. I sink deeper into the shelter of the cattails and shiver, wishing for the afghan that's back in the car. The damp is seeping into the seat of my Levis, and my backside is getting numb. I slip my hands into my pockets, flexing them for warmth.

The sky darkens—but not only from the dusk. Suddenly, the air is filled with the sound of hundreds of pairs of wings as squadrons of Canada geese appear. Their downy breasts look bloody, reflecting the rays of the now-scarlet sunset. Waves and waves of geese, shaped like bowling pins with feathers, honking. They blacken the sky above me and then land with precision in open areas of the marsh.

Impulsively, I cower down in the cattails. Where has this conflagration of geese come from? Every soccer field, retention pond, golf course, and playground in Glen Ellyn must have emptied itself of avian life to contribute to this gathering. Like the black, obsessive thoughts that won't be banished from my mind, they come to settle on the marsh for the night, entrenched, omnipresent.

Dark thoughts. They crowd in like the geese. The unkind words. The unhappiness I feel. The bitterness that is setting in, affecting me far more than it is the person who vented his anger at me and humiliated me. He has forgotten the incident already, I'm sure. I'm the one who is agonizing. Angry. Hating.

What broken vessels we are! What fragile pieces of pottery. We are shattered by things most would see as trivial. Why does God choose to let us be broken—our edges sharp, our hands bloody as we try to put the pieces back together? Does he hear us in our despair? Or does he turn his back, as he did when Christ was bloodied and broken for us on the cross?

How together we think we are, our lives under control, only to be torn up by a passing remark, a chance circumstance. Bludgeoned by a death. Annihilated by an accident. Wounded by words.

No one knows our secret hurts. We are masters of disguise, experts in cover-up. We hide things well. How fabulous our facades. How tightly the mask of falsehood adheres to our true selves.

Hatred. Bitterness. Anger. They can all be, well, so temporarily satisfying. John Ortberg mulls this over in *The Life*

You've Always Wanted, when he admits, "I cannot pray for very long without my mind drifting into a fantasy of angry revenge over some past slight I thought I had long since forgiven."

I know that the consequences of not letting go of these emotions are serious. In *Notes of a Native Son*, James Baldwin is aghast at his simmering hatred when he finds himself exploding in rage, ready to commit murder. It brings him face to face with himself: "I saw nothing very clearly, but I did see this: that my life, my *real* life, was in danger, and not from anything other people might do but from the hatred I carried in my own heart. . . . Hatred, which could destroy so much, never failed to destroy the man who hated."

The growing darkness is now a mist that blurs the colors around me into shades of gray. The clamor of the geese fades to a murmur as they settle down for the night, tucking their bills into their wings to rest. The cover of blackness is almost complete.

I feel God peeling off my layers—my anger, my bitterness—like the dragon in C. S. Lewis's *Voyage of the Dawn Treader* shedding its skin. I remember that the dragon's skin was not peeled off all at one time. Rather, it came off in layers and layers and layers of false skins. Layers of bitterness, layers of anger, layers of hate, all painfully skinned off.

So many never-ending layers. How long must I endure this scraping of my soul?

I pray for release from this hatred. I pray for the person who wronged me. My mind rebels, though, and the words I need to speak in forgiveness won't come. The spirit is willing, but

125

my will to forgive is not. Sighing, I give up, give it to God. I'm not able to forgive right now, but God can cover it. We've been down this route before. It will take many of these times of giving it to God, consigning my "friend" to prayer every time his name crosses my mind, before I can truly forgive.

In *The Quiet Answer*, Hugh Prather reminds me how he forgives:

> I release you from my hurt feelings. I free you from my read-ing of your motives. I withdraw my "justified" outrage and leave you clean and happy in my mind. In place of censure, I offer you all of God's deep contentment and peace.

Now really, God, this is too much. I may forgive him, but I would like him to suffer a little bit. Okay, maybe a lot. Let him suffer a lot. After all, he really wronged me. I fume. I revisit my hurt feelings. God, this is so unfair.

Do I really have to leave him "clean and happy" in my mind?

I'm going to have to wait a while for forgiveness to be my honest desire. At the moment, I don't want to let go of this hatred. But I make every effort, and I know, with the certainty of past experience, it will get easier. The shell is starting to crack. The layers are starting to peel.

Again, James Baldwin helps me understand my stubborn-ness, my clutching at the wrong done to me: "I imagine that one of the reasons people cling to their hates so stubbornly is because they sense, once hate is gone, that they will be forced to deal with pain." I don't want to deal with any more pain. I want to throw up walls of hatred, of bitterness—anything to block the pain. I rise stiffly and sling on my pack. Trudging down the path to the car, I feel a dull ache.

The lateness of the hour makes the path difficult to see. As I walk the deer trail that runs by the lake, something large and ungainly bursts from a clump of cattails by the shore. Annoyed at my disturbance, a blue heron flaps off in awkward disarray, lumbering to a new resting spot across the lake and cursing me under his breath, no doubt, in colorful bird vocabulary. Unexpected beauty in the darkness.

Carlo Carretto's words echo through my thoughts: "Here is something new indeed. You might say that the very experience of pain has brought us something we did not have before. With pain comes nothing less than the knowledge of the Absolute."

I will cling to this thought. I want to know you, Lord. I will let go of my hatred, this darkness, and deal with the pain. Starting here. Starting now.

WHILE TRACKING

Looking for the Signs

Faith is the substance of things hoped for, the evidence of things not seen.

HEBREWS 11:1 KJV

128

There's been a fracas in the whitewashed landscape of January, a life and death battle on a windswept field of snow. I'm walking through the woods, and sunlight is glinting off the white drifts, caressing the evergreen branches over my head and illuminating the icy path ahead of me. The light is so clean, hard, and bright that it's difficult to see in the glare.

I'm following tracks across the newly fallen snow, checking for critters and breaking in a new book I recently purchased on the subject. The night has left frozen footprints on the trace, embedded in frost: long indentations, short smudges, odd tail marks—imprinted shadows left by things I can't see but I know are all around me.

My breath blows out smoky clouds in the sunlight, and my nose is numb. I gulp hot chocolate from my thermos, trying to send sweet warmth to the extremities of fingers and toes. I started the hike with my knitted face mask pulled over my head against the cold, but my Darth Vader–like breathing made the material unpleasantly damp and chilly against my face. Resigned, I pulled the face mask off and stuck it in my jacket pocket. Now my hair is mussed, my face numb in the refrigerated air, but I like the feeling of the sunlight hitting as much exposed skin as I can bear. In Chicago, you miss the sun in the winter months and make the most of the light when it makes a brief appearance. Although it's tempting to sit by the fireplace, I like throwing myself into the arms of the weather, embracing the snow, bearing the cold.

I follow the trail from the woods to the stream that acts like an umbilical cord, connecting the woods to the prairie. Under the bridge of Willoway Creek, the water is a cracked mirror. Bluegill swim torpidly under the ice—a winter aquarium of sorts. The snow has dusted the surface of the creek for prints.

Carefully stepping out on the suspended ice, testing it for stability, I bend over to investigate the animal autographs scrawled across the watercourse. I pick out the tracks of a muskrat, its hind prints long and hand-like, its front prints small and rounder. A tail drag line runs down the center of the prints. Habitat gives me a clue to their maker, since I know muskrats live by shallow water edges. The prints lead to a hollow in the banks.

I study my tracking book, trying to memorize the terms that will help me interpret what I see. Print. Track. Leap. Stride. In *Track Finder,* I can see how long each mammal print is, its shape, the most likely places it will be found. The book gives me confidence, helps me figure things out. It gives me some direction, some parameters for interpreting the signs. Without the book, I would wander around, trying to figure everything out on my own, making wrong guesses.

Up the banks and across the bridge, I start through the grassy fields. The snow here is marked as if a typist has gone off on a crazy jag. Minuscule impressions jiggle and jog all over the page of the landscape.

Meadow voles and white-footed deermice left most of the tiny tracks I see, but I despair of distinguishing between them, satisfying myself with lumping the diverse family into one group. Snow tunnels run from bluegrass clump to bluegrass clump, an icy prairie subway system, a mousy mass transit. There is silence all around me, but I can close my eyes and feel the hum of activity going on, invisible, unseen, shrouded in whiteness, muffled in frost.

My route takes me to a clearing in the dried grasses, and I stop short to read some scribbled hieroglyphics. The brush marks of feathers, short scratch marks of claws. Evidence of a red-tailed hawk's landing intersecting with the trail of a mouse, shrew, or vole. No blood. I wonder if the hawk got a carryout dinner or if the little deermouse made it back home to tell his family a hair-raising adventure tale: "There I was, just minding my own business, when suddenly, a shadow fell across the path. . . ."

Just ahead, someone else was not so lucky. On the other side of a snowdrift, a jumble of ebony and ivory feathers and a bright red smudge of blood on the pure white of the snow tell me a coyote had Canada goose for breakfast. Still-fresh scat in melting ice says the carnage was recent. I look around nervously, more alert. I move on quickly.

Sign, sign, everywhere a sign. . . .

I like to walk at a forest preserve close to my house, where I occasionally catch glimpses of beavers. Before I ever saw one, I saw the evidence: chewed stumps, toppled trees, a dam. For the most part, beavers stay concealed. Occasionally I'll

131

see wet noses held above water as they swim in the summer. I know they are still there in the winter due to their surfacing holes, perfect cookie-cutter circles in the icy creek. In their lodge in the dam, they sit around eating bark, whiling the winter days away.

Sometimes I watch quietly for a frozen hour, hoping one will surface at a hole, but all I see are bubbles rising under the ice. The presence of my collie running and barking alongside the bank more than likely deters them from appearing. Now I know why Annie Dillard never took a dog with her to Tinker Creek.

The signs change from season to season. In spring, a dampened groove left on the muddy bank of my pond shows me where a toad has sited his launching pad. No book helps me here, just the experience of knowing I have toads in my pond and occasionally seeing a blur of motion from that part of the bank.

In the summer, scratch marks from the claws of the striped skunk show me where she digs for grubs in my front lawn. I've never seen a striped skunk in my yard, but the evidence overwhelmingly supports it. My out-of-shape cat, Socks, has been convicted—up close and personal. The scent left her a living testimonial to the skunk's presence and banished from our laps for a six-week period.

On my hands and knees in the snow, I measure prints. Some tracks are easy to read, like the four-inch-long distinctive hoof marks of the white-tailed deer. Others are more difficult, such as figuring out the difference between gray fox and red fox prints.

Weather also plays a role in reading the signs. Tracks look different in snow than they do in, say, mud or sand.

Once I figure out the separate tracks, I can begin to construct the bigger picture, put things into context. The intersection of coyote tracks and feathers plus blood must equal dinner. Vole and hawk marks minus blood mean dinner was a near miss—or à la carte. The cloverleaf prints of busy mice and shrews crossing between snow tunnels shows activity going on just below the surface. Muskrat tracks under the bridge tell the story of someone out foraging for a little dinner.

"Be observant . . . ," says the book. I'm trying. Trying to pay attention. Trying to absorb a little knowledge from the book. Trying to learn to interpret what is visible and make guesses about what I can't see.

Some of the signs are challenging to decipher, paragraphs in stories I haven't learned to read yet. I don't have the vocabulary to understand them or the knowledge to interpret their meanings—even with the guidance of the book. Other signs I miss by not paying attention, by not being more observant. I know there are more complicated chronicles than the simple stories I read in a casual glance over the surface of the terrain.

The signs are there if I look for them. Evidence of things hoped for, yet unseen. I'm learning that there's more to this life than meets the eye. I'm consulting the book, taking some things on faith.

At the Feeder

Taking the Bad with the Good

[We must] accept what we very often cannot avoid, and endure with love and resignation things which could cause us weariness and disgust. This is what being holy means.

Jean-Pierre de Caussade

A chatter at the feeder awakens me. The sun hasn't cracked the horizon yet, but already a bird brawl is taking place right outside my open bedroom window, a feathered fight of colossal proportions.

I sigh, then turn over and pull the pillow over my head to block the sounds. Yesterday I put out a fresh batch of black oil sunflower seeds on the concrete ledge to placate the ongoing arguments between the birds over the rations I dish out daily in my backyard. Obviously, this has not helped suburban peace.

Although it's still dark, I can hear the birds establishing a breakfast pecking line at the five feeders hanging on my back porch. I enjoy having a variety of birds visit, so I read bird books and consult with bird store clerks to know just what kinds of munchies each species prefers. Thistle tempts the goldfinches. Sunflower seeds charm the cardinals. Ruby-colored feeders full of sugar water attract the hummers. Corn brings in the blue jays, and peanuts pull in the woodpeckers. A seedy smorgasboard, a fast-food festival.

But is this varied menu selection enough to keep the peace? Nooooo. Like quarreling toddlers, the blue jays think the cardinals have something better and flap over to drive them away from the sunflower seeds. Chickadees and woodpeckers bicker over the peanuts. There's a sparrow scrimmage in progress on the ledge. Raspberry-breasted house finches scold and flap around the seed dispensers. It's a feathered free-for-all.

A blush of dawn illumines the bedroom, and as it does, thoughts also come to light. I went to bed wrestling with a difficult relationship, and my last reflections before sleep are now my first thoughts in the morning. There's an unlovable person in my life, and I'm stuck with her.

I punch my pillow. I'm trying to love her, but I really dislike her a great deal at the moment. This person seems to have made it a personal mission to make my life a misery.

Lord, if I have to sit through another meeting with her, I'm going to jump out the second-floor window. God, what an albatross hangs around my neck.

Albatross, I muse. Don't have those at the feeder. The chattering is reaching a crescendo outside, and now the dog is up, looking from me to the closed bedroom door expectantly. I summon energy and groan my way out of bed. As I open the back door to put her out, the birds scatter to the neighbors' trees but keep a close watch on what I'm doing. After clipping the dog to her line, I return to the kitchen and grind some Irish Creme coffee, keeping one eye on the kitchen window. As the coffee begins to drip, I watch as the birds straggle back.

At the suet cage hanging outside the window over the sink, a woodpecker appears. He hangs on the mesh and pecks at the fatty mix. We're separated by only a few feet and some window screens as I pull my mug from the cabinet and fill it. Downy or hairy woodpecker? I mull it over. They are so similar. Hairys are bigger, I remind myself, and have a larger

136

bill. I squint at it, framing it with my mental measuring stick. About seven inches from head to tail. Downy, I decide.

I look past the woodpecker to the raucous blue jays, resplendent in their blue feathers trimmed in white lace. They are intent on stuffing themselves at the squirrel-resistant peanut feeder. An occasional black-capped chickadee takes his turn when he finds the feeder unoccupied by the brawnier bullies.

Goldfinches are abundant this morning, olive and lemon drops perched upside down on the thistle feeder, with its mini dispensing holes repelling undesirables. The sunflower feeder is full of house finches.

On the ground, cardinals, garish as holly berries, mingle in pleasing contrast with sober mourning doves, moving sedately like nuns in their cloaks of softest gray, foraging for dropped seeds from the feeder.

I try to attract an assortment of birds. Yet, into this collection of fair-weather friends, a few storm clouds blow.

Starlings.

And here they come. Iridescent in the early morning sunshine, they are freckled with white "stars" and sport yellow or brown bills. There's a departing flurry of feathers at the feeder as the starlings move in, taking over. The starlings' mixed chirps and twitters mimic the bird songs of the other diners they are driving away, mocking them as they casually finish the leftovers.

Introduced to America from Europe and Asia in the late 1800s, the starling outmuscles native birds for nesting holes, contributing to the decline of several species of birds in North

America. Chunky, brawny, and a bully in the bird world, it clears out the colorful array of birds at my feeder with its unwelcome appearances. When starlings show up, the other birds retreat to neighboring trees as fast as customers run from a health warning tacked up at a local restaurant.

Right behind them are the sparrows. There are many species of sparrows, but they all look alike to me. Field sparrow, song sparrow, chipping sparrow, tree sparrow. Little brown jobs, some of the books call them, although an ecology professor I know assures me they are easily distinguishable by eye rings and tail feathers. Ha! Easy for her to say.

They flock to my feeders with insatiable appetites, amass in the neighbors' willow that overhangs the fence, then make an assault by air on the concrete ledge. Their kissing cousins, the juncos, also join these family reunions, jostling for seed that falls on the patio.

It's the house sparrows that have kept me from building a bluebird box. Like illegal squatters, the little brown guys would take them over and build nests. I would then have to patrol the boxes and kick out the sparrows to make room for the bluebirds.

God knows when even one sparrow drops to the ground, so I don't dare mess with them. I've decided to stick with bird feeders.

Sometimes I wonder if God had an off day when he made some of these species. I still haven't figured out where they fit in. What was on his mind when he whipped up a starling, put together a house sparrow?

And then there are the squirrels. Undesirable interlopers. So cute, so fuzzy, flicking their tails, thumbing their squirrel noses at me, raiding my seed supply. To add insult to injury, they find new ways to break into my expensive squirrel-proof feeders and chomp the cheaper plastic ones to bits. They hang upside down on my squirrel-resistant peanut feeder, gnawing at nuts through the green mesh. Others plan their invasion from strategic positions on the roof. On their way to the all-you-can-eat seed buffet, they wreak havoc in the garden, sampling tomatoes, crunching on tender plants.

I sigh. I can't help liking them despite their destructive behavior. They have their moments—the baby fox squirrel that entertains us with his antics, the big, muscular gray squirrel that sits in the rain, munching on corn, with his tail flipped over his back and head like a furry, bottle-brush umbrella.

I've made my peace with the squirrels—for the most part anyway. I even hammered together a homemade perch with a nailed-on piece of corn to lure them away from the bird seed. Of course, it just attracted more squirrels. Word in the trees must spread fast. Our yard is now as popular to them as a well-lit truck stop in Nebraska is to truck drivers.

Most of the wildlife in my small backyard is familiar, but once in a while something startling happens. I'm on the phone, and my daughter comes running into my home office, signaling frantically. She's been told to interrupt me only if there is an emergency, so I immediately put my client on hold and look at her questioningly.

139

"There's a new bird at the feeder!" she says, dancing from foot to foot.

This qualifies as an emergency in my book. Immediately, I tell the client I need to call him back and race to the kitchen window with her.

Sure enough, fluttering around the feeders is a bright green parakeet—definitely not in my field guide to North American birds. A surprise addition to my feathered menagerie. I wonder whose cage the parakeet escaped from and how it will handle the harsh Chicago winter just around the bend. It seems happy to be outdoors, flocking together with some house finches. I wonder how they tolerate each other, how the finches accept this exotic into their midst, how the parakeet accepts its drabber country relations.

The birds outside my windows offer an ever changing, always fascinating drama as I go about my daily tasks. I'm trying to suffer the starlings with the chickadees, stomach the squirrels with the woodpeckers, take the crows with the finches—and enjoy the occasional unexpected visitor that doesn't fit.

Accepting the unacceptable. Taking the good with the bad.

I think about the wearisome person in my life. I think about building character. It's difficult to love the unlovable, forgive those who don't ask for it, be vulnerable with those who occasionally ravage my spirit, trample my tranquillity. But it's the worst people who challenge me to go deeper, to build new reservoirs of strength, to draw on new sources for help.

Thomas à Kempis reminds me to "take pains to be patient in bearing the faults and weaknesses of others, for you too have many flaws that others must put up with."

I muse on this. I have many flaws my friends patiently endure. I forget to call. I'm selfish with my time. I'm moody, disorganized, and often run late for our get-togethers.

Maybe I'm going to accept a few starlings at my feeder. Their plumage is rather pretty, once you get over their personalities. I'll roll out the red carpet for the sparrows. Despite their voracious appetites, they are cheerful and pleasant, and some of their songs are beautiful. I'll even welcome a few squirrels, repairing the damage they leave in their wake.

I'm looking forward to seeing how everything shakes out. To see what shows up. To embrace the occasional oddball. To become more tolerant. Even if I don't always like it.

SANCTUARY

Restored by the Light

There are simply no answers to some of the great pressing questions. You continue to live them out, making your life a worthy expression of a leaning into the light.

BARRY LOPEZ

Rain pelts the house. It's the middle of the night, and I can't get back to sleep. I lie awake, listening to the storm, tossing and turning, worrying over old grievances and disappointments like a dog worries over a bone.

My pillow is soaked with tears. Restlessness stalks me like a shadow. Where is God in these dark nights of the soul? The rain hits the house in a wave, a deluge that shows no signs of stopping. I spend the rest of the night staring at the ceiling, then pass into a light sleep just as dawn begins to flush through the house.

Waking, weary, I rise with the alarm, get the kids off to school, then blindly reach for my hip pack. Some internal compass points me in the direction of my secret refuge without conscious thought or intention.

There is a place I go when everything in my world is turned upside down, when nothing I believe in makes sense anymore. It is a secret place, a place of renewing, a place of peace, a refuge when my mind and soul are sick with disappointment and despair.

This morning I am in need of my quiet place. I walk a quarter mile down a rutted asphalt road, then tread the shaded path through the savanna, a treasure chest of white oak and hickories. My sleep-deprived eyes take in the wet humus floor, delicately dotted with a patchwork of spring jewels—waxy yellow buttercups, cinnamon-copper trilliums, amethyst dog-tooth violets, all flanked by the intricate emerald lace of new growth. Cloven hoof prints of deer etch the muddy path like fleurs-de-lis, and pools of chocolate-milk rainwater dot the trail, a result of the storm the night before. The sky is sapphire blue, washed clean by the squall.

Despite the beauty all around me, my steps slow. Painful memories. Discouraging thoughts. They cling to my steps and mock me as I trudge along the path. Ghosts of past wrongs, hopelessness, loneliness, fear. I feel oppressed. The mud pulls at my hiking boots, sucking me downward with each step. The clammy coolness of the savanna feels like a tomb. My feet drag, crunching the moist gravel on the rutted path.

Suddenly, I emerge into bright sunshine. I squint into the light, temporarily blinded after the gloom. Spread out at the edge of the savanna is a hundred-acre prairie, a tableau of green grasses interwoven with wildflowers. Through the prairie runs the free-form blue squiggle of a meandering creek, which, despite the previous night's mayhem, runs azure and clear.

I walk faster, fueled by sunlight. I head for the bridge that spans the water and stretch out full-length on the wet concrete warming in the sunshine. Solar heat toasts my body. The wind blows softly through the grasses surrounding the creek, then ruffles my hair.

Peace. Stillness. Tranquillity.

A silvery blue heron fishes nearby and stands guard while I half doze, exhausted from my late-night wrestling match

144

with despair. High above, a dun-flecked song sparrow sings for his mate, filling his throat with a heartbreakingly beautiful aria that spills out onto the breeze and drifts through my reverie.

I bask in sunshine, taking in the world through scrunched-up eyes. A glimmer nearby catches my attention. Amid the newly budded leaves on the bur oak limbs that overhang the bridge, the light catches a mourning cloak flexing its wings. Open-winged, the butterfly is ebony and iridescent, each wing rimmed with blue dots, the jagged edges crusted with gold. Its drab, matte-finished underside camouflages it against the bark of the tree when its wings are folded, yet its beautiful interior wings glisten in the sun.

The undersides of nature—drab, yet concealing something of beauty, something of glory. Something hidden, something to be discovered. So much seen, so much unseen.

Stretching stiffly, I jump to my feet and move closer to the oak to investigate the mourning cloak. Two red-winged blackbirds protest my approach, scolding me, hovering around my head, wings flapping madly. "Trespasser!" they accuse, as I venture too close to their nest. I make a wide circle around them, keeping a polite distance, giving them space.

The wind blows gently, wafting the smell of the newly opened peach and white honeysuckle flowers to my nose and sidetracking me from my butterfly investigation. I inhale the floral fragrance greedily, and the perfume saturates me. Pausing, I strip off a white blossom and break the end open, pulling the pistil out through the bottom of the bloom. A single drop of nectar, untouched by bees, glistens. Tentatively, I touch it to the tip of my tongue. Ambrosia.

The grasses around me ripple and wave. The wind moving through them beats with the rhythmic hush of surf upon the shore. The creek trickles on its journey to nowhere, warbling in harmony with the song sparrow's clear notes. Light sparkles on the water, turning the surface into glittering diamonds.

I long for light, to absorb light, to immerse myself in it. I tug off my hiking boots, scrabble down the wet bank, and wade out into the creek, mud squishing through my toes, water spattering my rolled-up jeans. The light makes looking glasses of the quiet, small pools under the bur oak's roots, reflecting the petals of purple phlox lining the creek bank, picking out shiny mica embedded in rocks and stones. Colors blend in a crazy wet mishmash of moss greens, nut browns, intense violets, and blue sky the tint of the sea, now reflected in the placid water. Ankle deep in water, I stir it with my fingertips, churning the pigments together in a whirlpooled rainbow. Bending over, I cup the liquid in my palms and splash my face.

The hot sun warms my wet cheeks as I raise my face to the sky. Sunlight burns red through my closed eyelids, particles of light glistening, charging my body with warmth and energy.

I wade to the creek bank and sit on the muddy edge, wiggling my feet dry in the sunshine. I feel the tension drain out of me and flow into the creek—washed away in the light, blending with the myriad colors mirrored in the water.

146

Sprawling full-length, I try to get comfortable amid the dried goldenrod stalks and last year's moldering oak leaves. Turning over, I lie on my back and break off a spongy mushroom, twirling the fungus umbrella between my fingers. High above me, three red-tailed hawks catch the wind currents, playing tag with a coal-black crow and shrieking in unselfconscious joy. Spring peepers in the flooded meadow behind me sing a creaky chorus in unison.

Something in my memory stirs. My mind sings with the psalmist, "LORD, *who may dwell in your sanctuary? Who may live on your holy hill?"*

Me, Lord. Oh, let it be me. Let me live in your sanctuary. Let me lie on your holy hill. Grant me vision to see how each piece of my life fits into your larger plan. Let me rest in your comforting embrace and take refuge under your wings.

There are many epiphanies in my sanctuary. I think about a late spring evening as I walk the wetlands. I stand, hidden, watching a great egret fishing. Unaware of my eyes on him, he stretches his snake-like neck as if for the pleasure of the movement itself. He is blinding white against the spring's new-green growth of cattails and canary grass. His orange bill, crisp and scissors-sharp, suddenly plunges into the watery muck, and he brings up a fish, fighting for life in his pincer-like grasp. Water sprays through the air in glistening droplets. Gulping, the egret swallows, the shape of the thrashing fish moving in lumps and humps against his skinny neck as it goes down, down, down. Satisfied, he stands poised, alert, gazing into the distance. A sudden move on my part, and the egret stretches his snowy wings, angel-like under the slanting shadows of the sinking sun, and sweeps away.

Death. Life. Struggle. Beauty.

Closing my eyes, I remember a late February evening when I walked the gravel path, flanked by sentinels of dried Indian grass and big bluestem on the prairie. Over the murmur of the wind in the grasses, I hear a soft, high-pitched whisper overhead. Twenty-eight cedar waxwings sit in a black walnut tree, illuminated by the sunset, softly chiming a celebration of the day's end with their "Seep! Seep! Seep!" Creamy butter-gold bellies, polished and soft, blend into spiky, gel-tufted chestnut heads. Each tail is dipped in lemon yellow; a red splotch splashes each wing. Their bead-black eyes are rimmed with white racing stripes. Together, a vast, feathered choir robed in saffron, they sing an enchanting lullaby welcoming the growing twilight.

Holy, holy, holy.

Come Holy Spirit, come to this holy place. Bring your light to the gathering darkness.

I turn over on my mattress of old leaves and green shoots and smell the rain-soaked earth, rubbing it against my cheek.

"The boundary lines have fallen for me in pleasant places. . . . You have made known to me the path of life; you will fill me with joy in your presence, with eternal pleasures at your right hand."

Cover me with your wings. Let me rest in the peace of your sanctuary.

Sitting up, I stretch my arms toward the sun, rejoicing. The bitter memories of the night have been erased. The sun has evaporated the storms that raged in me only hours before. I am now at peace, baptized by the water of the creek, seared clean by sunlight. I pull on my hiking boots, pick up my pack, and head for home.

NOTES

Introduction

p. 9. John Ortberg, *The Life You've Always Wanted* (Grand Rapids: Zondervan, 1997), 8.

p. 11. The spiral patterns on the faces of sunflowers are arranged according to the Fibonacci series, named after an Italian mathematician who discovered that an ideal geometrical proportion exists in many plants and shells. If you count the florets in a sunflower, you will find that each number is the sum of the two that precedes it (i.e., 1, 1, 2, 3, 5, 8, 13, 21, etc.). If you divide each number by the number that follows it (1/2, 2/3, 3/5, 5/8, etc.), you will find a ratio of .618, or "The Divine Proportion." This is detailed in an essay by Oliver Sacks, "Brilliant Light," in *The Best American Science and Nature Writing 2000*, ed.

David Quammen (New York: Houghton Mifflin, 2000), 179–208.

p. 12. Evelyn Underhill, *Practical Mysticism* (England: Eagle Books, 1991), 10.

p. 13. Søren Kierkegaard, *The Prayers of Kierkegaard*, ed. Perry LeFebre (Chicago: University of Chicago, 1956), 10.

Chapter 1

p. 15. Stephen Plant, *Great Christian Thinkers: Simone Weil*, ed. Peter Vardy (Liguori, Mo.: Ligouri Publications, 1997), 13, quoting Simone Weil, *Gravity and Grace* (London: HarperCollins Religious, 1987).

Chapter 2

p. 26. The Paul Gauguin painting "Where do we come from? What are we? Where are we going?" is on display in the Musee des Arts Africans

151

et Oceaniens, Paris, France. It is referenced in Richard Brettell, *Gauguin* (Washington, D.C.: National Gallery of Art, 1988), 23.

p. 28. "Cold-hearted orb . . .": Graham Edge, "Morning Glory," in the song "Nights in White Satin," recorded by The Moody Blues (Universal Music Group, 1967).

p. 28. Joseph Conrad, quoted in Robert I. Fitzhenry, ed., *Harper Book of Quotations,* 3d ed. (New York: HarperCollins, 1993), 24.

pp. 29–30. Carlo Carretto, *Why O Lord? The Inner Meaning of Suffering,* trans. Robert R. Barr (Maryknoll, N.Y.: Orbis Books, 1986), 25.

p. 30. The planetarium artist, Edwin Faughn, was profiled in "Finding God in the Heavens," *Life@Work Journal* 2, no. 3 (May/June 1999): 26.

pp. 30–31. Bret Lott, from an original essay, copyright Bret Lott.

p. 32. Teresa of Avila, *The Interior Castle,* quoted in Robert Benson, *Living Prayer* (New York: Jeremy Tarcher, 1998), 27. The classic translation is "Alas, O Lord, to what a state dost thou bring those who love thee!" but I like the vernacular better.

p. 32. Timothy Ferris, *The Whole Shebang* (New York: Simon & Schuster, 1997), 27.

p. 32. Carl Sagan, quoted in Fitzhenry, *Harper Book of Quotations,* 28.

p. 32. Psalm 8:3–4.

p. 33. Barry Lopez, *Arctic Dreams* (New York: Charles Scribner and Sons, 1986), 28.

Chapter 3

p. 35. Anatole France, quoted in Robert I. Fitzhenry, ed., *Harper Book of Quotations,* 3d ed. (New York: HarperCollins, 1993), 31.

p. 36. C. S. Lewis, *The Magician's Nephew* (New York: HarperCollins, 1994), 31.

Chapter 4

p. 43. Wendell Berry, "October 11," in *Selected Poems of Wendell Berry* (Washington, D.C.: Counterpoint, 1998), 39.

Portions of this chapter were influenced by two wonderful books: an essay by Parker Palmer, "Autumn," in *Let Your Life Speak: Listening for the Voice of Vocation* (San Francisco: Jossey-Bass Publishers, 2000), and fall entries in Mary Blocksma, *Naming Nature: A Seasonal Guide for the Amateur Naturalist* (New York: Penguin, 1992).

Chapter 5

p. 50. Juan Ramon Jimenez, quoted in Robert I. Fitzhenry, ed., *Harper Book of Quotations,* 3d ed. (New York: HarperCollins, 1993), 45.

p. 51. My neighbor Gerould "Gerry" Wilhelm is the coauthor with Floyd Swink of *Plants of the Chicago Region* (Indianapolis: Indiana Academy of Sciences, 1994).

p. 53. Jane Kenyon, *A Hundred White Daffodils* (St. Paul, Minn.: Graywolf Press, 1999), 48.

p. 55. Robert Benson uses this phrase in *Living Prayer* (New York: Jeremy Tarcher, 1998), 47.

p. 56. Walter Brueggemann, *The Land as Promise* (Minneapolis: Fortress, 1977), 49.

Chapter 6

p. 57. William Johnston, *The Cloud of Unknowing* (New York: Doubleday, 1973), 146.

p. 59. Jane Kenyon, *A Hundred White Daffodils* (St. Paul, Minn.: Graywolf Press, 1999), 52.

pp. 63–64. Ibid., 56.

Chapter 7

p. 65. Rainer Maria Rilke, "Letter No. 4," in *Letters to a Young Poet*, trans. M. D. Herter (New York: Norton, 1934, 1935), 59.

p. 67. The original story about the homesteaders, "Living the Dream" by Deanna Kawatski, was published in *Mother Earth News* (August/September 1991): 60.

p. 68. Georgia O'Keeffe, quoted in Laurie Lisle, *Portrait of an Artist:*

A Biography of Georgia O'Keeffe (New York: Washington Square Press, 1997), 61.

Chapter 8

p. 72. Evelyn Underhill, *Practical Mysticism* (England: Eagle Books, 1991), 66.

p. 76. The description of the brown recluse spider is from Lorus and Margery Milne, *National Audubon Society Field Guide to North American Insects and Spiders* (New York: Alfred A. Knopf, 1998), 69.

Chapter 9

p. 81. Thomas à Kempis, *The Imitation of Christ: A Timeless Classic for Contemporary Readers*, trans. William C. Creasy (Notre Dame, Ind.: Ave Maria Press, 1989), 74.

p. 86. John Ortberg, *The Life You've Always Wanted* (Grand Rapids: Zondervan, 1997), 77.

Chapter 10

p. 88. Thomas Berry, quoted in April N. Rieveschl, "Spirals," in *American Nature Writing*, ed. John A. Murray (San Francisco: Sierra Club Books, 1998), 81.

p. 90. Sue Monk Kidd, *When the Heart Waits* (New York: Harper & Row, 1990), 82.

p. 92. Jan DeBlieu, *Wind* (New York: Houghton Mifflin, 1998), 84.

Chapter 11

p. 96. Bruce Cockburn, "Christmas Song," *Salt, Sun and Time* (Toronto: Golden Mountain Music Corporation, 1974).

p. 98. John Madsen's classic work, *Where the Sky Began: Land of the Tallgrass Prairie* (Ames, Ia.: Iowa State University Press, 1995), is a great read for more information and inspiration about this vanishing ecosystem.

Chapter 12

p. 104. Nicholas Wolterstorff, *Lament for a Son* (Grand Rapids: Eerdmans, 1987), 96.

pp. 106–7. The poem is from Edna St. Vincent Millay, "Renascence," in *Collected Poems,* ed. Norma Millay (New York: HarperCollins, 1912, 1940), 97.

pp. 108, 111. Brooks Williams, "Night Fears," *Knife Edge* (Hamilton, Ont.: Grant Avenue Studio, 1995).

p. 111. Teresa of Avila, *Beyond Suffering,* entries for Day 37 and Day 38, quoted in John Kirvan, *That You May Have Life: Let the Mystics Be Your Guide for Lent* (Notre Dame, Ind.: Ave Maria Press, 1998), 102.

Chapter 13

p. 117. Thomas à Kempis, *The Imitation of Christ: A Timeless Classic for Contemporary Readers,* trans. William C. Creasy (Notre Dame, Ind.: Ave Maria Press, 1989), 106.

Chapter 14

p. 121. Henri J. M. Nouwen, *The Inner Voice of Love* (New York: Doubleday, 1996), 112.

pp. 124–25. John Ortberg, *The Life You've Always Wanted* (Grand Rapids: Zondervan, 1997), 114.

p. 125. James Baldwin, *Notes of a Native Son* (Boston: Beacon Press, 1990), 114.

p. 125. C. S. Lewis, *The Voyage of the Dawn Treader* (New York: HarperCollins, 1994), 115.

p. 126. Hugh Prather, *The Quiet Answer* (New York: Doubleday, 1982), 115.

pp. 126–27. Baldwin, *Notes of a Native Son,* 116.

p. 127. Carlo Carretto, *Why O Lord? The Inner Meaning of Suffering,* trans. Robert R. Barr (Maryknoll, N.Y.: Orbis Books, 1986), 116.

Chapter 15

p. 130. This indispensable little book, *Track Finder,* by Dorcas Miller, is available from the Nature Study Guild Publishers, P.O. Box 10489, Rochester, NY 14610-0489, or www.naturestudy.com.

p. 132. Annie Dillard's *Pilgrim at Tinker Creek* (New York: Harper-

154

Collins, 1974), chapter 11, is a lovely essay about the art of watching muskrats.

Chapter 16

p. 134. Jean-Pierre de Caussade, *Abandonment to Divine Providence*, quoted in *A Guide to Prayer for All God's People*, ed. Rueben P. Job (Nashville: Upper Room Books, 1990), 124.

p. 141. Thomas à Kempis, *The Imitation of Christ: A Timeless Classic for Contemporary Readers*, trans. William C. Creasy (Notre Dame, Ind.: Ave Maria Press, 1989), 129.

Jon L. Dunn, *The National Geographic Field Guide to Birds of North America*, 3d ed. (Washington, D.C.: National Geographic Society, 1999), is my personal favorite for amateur birding. If you like photos rather than drawings, try Donald and Lillian Stokes, *Stokes Field Guide to Birds* (New York: Little, Brown and Company, 1996).

Chapter 17

p. 142. Barry Lopez, *Arctic Dreams* (New York: Charles Scribner and Sons, 1986), 132.

p. 147. Psalm 15:1.

p. 148. Psalm 16:6, 11.

ACKNOWLEDGMENTS

This book would not have been possible without the help and encouragement of the following people:

My family: Jeff, who thought I could, even when I didn't—I love you!; Dustin and Jennifer, who put up with late nights and long hours; my mom, Carolyn Strafford, who gave me the keys to the outdoors, and my dad, Bill Strafford, who taught me to question; my grandparents, George and Lois Page, who showed me how to clean a fish, bait a hook, and always had time; Nancy Crosby, my other mom and my cheerleader; and my siblings, Sherry Rediger and Chris Strafford—thanks for the memories.

A few friends: Vinita Hampton Wright, advisor extraordinaire, for always having the right blend of suggestions and praise; Lil Copan, who gave me Jane Kenyon and a kick in the seat of the pants; Alice Fryling, who jump-started the batteries; Robert Benson, who prodded me to write out of my brokenness; Margo Smith, who always had the words I needed at the right time; Terry Glaspey and Carolyn McCready, who

157

affirmed and encouraged; and Phyllis Tickle, who sets a shining example.

Other friends at Baker Book House: Dan and Ann Baker for all their kind words; Dwight Baker, who introduced me to the prairie, shared books, and answered endless questions; Tamara Baker for being the messenger of good news; Dave Lewis, Don Stephenson, and Melinda Van Engen for their support. Special thanks to Bob Hosack for going the extra mile.

Many, many thanks also to Gerould and Margaret Wilhelm and Dave Wilhelm for their generosity in sharing their knowledge and their plants; and James T. Flynn, "Jim," for all the wonderful vegetables. Thanks, neighbors!

The following folks were kind enough to review the manuscript in whole or in part. Any remaining errors are my own responsibility: Gerould Wilhelm, coauthor of *Plants of the Chicago Region*; the visitors center staff at the Barataria Preserve of Jean Lafitte National Historical Park and Preserve in Louisiana, for their help in ensuring that I didn't call a swamp a bog and a wax myrtle a cypress; the Burpee Seed Company customer service desk staff, who researched their catalogs from the sixties; Jeffrey Skibins, manager of natural history education, the Morton Arboretum, Lisle, Illinois; Ron Garbers, naturalist and night sky instructor at the Morton Arboretum; and James Ballowe, nature writing instructor at the Morton Arboretum, who critiqued some early essays.

And a very special thanks to the staff at Caribou Coffee in Glen Ellyn, Illinois, who fixed me hundreds of vanilla mochas while I worked at "my" table for hours on end: Andy, Barb, Beth, Carolyn, Krissy, Daniel, Erika, Heather, Jen, Jodi, John, Mallory, Megan, Nicky, Sara, Sarah, Shawny, and Susie. Hey guys—thanks for the extra whipped cream!

Cindy Crosby is a full-time freelance writer whose work has appeared in numerous publications, including *Publishers Weekly*, *PW Religion BookLine*, *Christianity Today*, *Today's Christian Woman*, and *Marriage Partnership*. She loves baseball, making cheesecake from scratch, and listening to Van Morrison, and hates gray days and housework. When she's not reading, hiking, or working in the garden, she likes to hang out at the local coffee shop, looking for caffeinated inspiration for her writing. She and her husband, Jeff, are former independent bookstore owners and the parents of two teenagers, Dustin and Jennifer. They live in Glen Ellyn, Illinois. This is Cindy's first book.